Indian Soci

INDIAN SOCIOLOGY from Where to Where

Footnotes to the History of the Discipline

Yogesh Atal

RAWAT PUBLICATIONS
Jaipur • New Delhi • Bangalore • Hyderabad • Guwahati

ISBN 978-81-7033-760-7

Reprinted, 2025

Published by
Prem Rawat for **Rawat Publications**
Satyam Apts., Sector 3, Jawahar Nagar, Jaipur - 302 004 (India)
Phone: 0141 265 1748 / 7006 E-mail : info@rawatbooks.com
Website: rawatbooks.com

New Delhi Office
4858/24, Ansari Road, Daryaganj, New Delhi 110 002
Phone: 011-23263290

Also at *Bangalore, Guwahati* and *Kolkata*

Typeset by Rawat Computers, Jaipur
Printed at Nice Printing Press, New Delhi

Contents

Preface

The essays assembled in this book were written on different occasions during my long career in the profession that began in 1959. Both as a teacher and a research administrator, in India and abroad, I got several opportunities to reflect on the growth of sociology and anthropology in India. My assignments with the Indian Council of Social Science Research and UNESCO demanded continuous reflection on the developing trends in the two disciplines. As the first UNESCO Regional Adviser for Social and Human Sciences in Asia and the Pacific I had the good fortune of acquainting myself with the social science developments in the region and of assisting in their further growth. This exposure gave me a comparative perspective to view Indian social science. I found it useful to follow the framework of sociology of social science rather than concentrate on mere chronology of events.

Of the several pieces I had written and published in the past forty years on the growth of social sciences and sociology, I have selected thirteen that are relevant to Indian sociology to be reproduced here in a book form. Thus, at one place, my way of looking at the growth of Indian sociology will be available to those who care.

All of these essays, save two, have been published earlier. Both of the unpublished essays were delivered as speeches at important sociological gatherings in India. The brief essay on

"Social Transformation" was delivered as a Keynote Address at the National Seminar organized by the Panjab University, Chandigarh in March 2000. The other essay, with which this book concludes, is a post-factum pen-down version of a brief oral statement made at the All-India Sociological Conference held at Amritsar to mark the Golden Jubilee of the founding of the Indian Sociological Society in December 2001. It is a fitting conclusion to this collection.

Written as independent essays and at different points of time, the discerning reader is sure to find differences in writing style, and to notice shifting emphases. But the reader may also witness the growth of a professional, with his ideas or viewpoints becoming clearer and refined over time. The earliest essay was written sometime in 1961, only two years after I joined the profession. Some others were written as "Addresses". I have retained their format even when these have some autobiographical hints—at my age, I can afford that little indulgence, I hope.

The essay on "Sociology and the Future" was delivered as a Valedictory Address to the 1984 All India Sociological Conference held at Vadodara. But somehow it never found a place in the *Sociological Bulletin*—the official organ of the Indian Sociological Society. However, it was published in the *International Social Science Journal* and got translated into Spanish, French, and Chinese. The paper titled, "Sociology in the Indian Campus" was originally written at the request of the organizers of the All-India Sociological Conference, held in Varanasi, but was published in the first volume of *Main Currents in Indian Sociology*, edited by Professor Giri Raj Gupta of the University of Western Illinois, Macomb, USA. Strangely enough, the two-three collections of essays relative to Indian sociology published at the time of the World Conference of Sociology, held in India, did not include any of my essays on Indian sociology for whatever they are worth. The point I am making is that the selectivity in the profession has a "social" (or, call it "political") dimension. Recognizing this, I thought that, at least for the record, I must make available my writings at one place for the future historian of the discipline.

The collection contains first two essays on the general social science scene in the region of the Asia and the Pacific. These should help the reader to locate the Indian case better. Also included are two of my essays that have attracted worldwide attention and have been translated into several languages, and are also included in some anthologies and books of readings. One relates to the call for indigenization of social sciences. Readers will recall that a special session was held at the World Conference of Sociology, held in India, to discuss the question of indigenization where all inputs were in the form of commentaries on my essay published earlier by the *International Social Science Journal.* This session was convened by Professor Fred Riggs, then Chairperson of COCTA (Committee on Conceptual and Terminological Analysis) of the International Social Science Council. A post-conference seminar was also organized in Jaipur on the same theme under the joint auspices of COCTA and the Indian Council of Social Science Research (ICSSR).

I must add that as UNESCO Social Science Adviser I took the initiative in convening a discussion during the AASSREC (The Association of Asia-Pacific Social Science Research Councils) Conference, held in Manila in 1980 on the issue of Indigenization of Social Sciences. My paper, titled "The Call for Indigenization", was an outcome of that discussion and was written as an introduction to the booklet containing the proceedings of that discussion and published by the International Federation of Social Science Organizations (IFSSO). I edited it in collaboration with Jan Loubser of IFSSO. My paper was also published in the *International Social Science Journal.* Twenty years after that event, during which the debate was taken further the world over, the University of Singapore organized an Asian Seminar in 1998 to review the process of indigenization. As initiator of the debate on indigenization, I was invited to that meeting. I used that opportunity to reflect on indigenization of Indian sociology. Both these papers are reproduced here, although the original paper is more conceptual.

Another conceptual essay is on the use of social sciences for policy. Since it was written for the volume honouring Professor M.V. Mathur, it is more interdisciplinary in character but of interest to sociologists as well. This paper has also been published in the *International Social Science Journal* and translated into several languages.

This volume contains my essay on village studies in India. The trend of village studies began in the fifties in India and became a distinguishing trait of Indian sociology. Now that rural studies have somehow receded in the background, it is important for newcomers in sociology to know about this important period in the history of Indian sociology. Hopefully, this might instigate some scholars to revive this branch of our discipline.

I have also included the paper that I recently prepared on the research priorities in education as Director-General of the Indian Institute of Education, Pune. I convened a meeting of experts drawn from different social science disciplines, and education, to draw up an agenda for social science research on education. The paper summarizes the outcome of that discussion and outlines an agenda for research on education. I am confident that this will encourage our young researchers to take up research projects to enrich sociology of education in this country.

This volume would not have been possible without the continuous persuasion by Shri Kailash Rawat of Rawat Publications. I am grateful to him for his appreciation of my work, and his decision to publish it.

Yogesh Atal

1

Development of Social Sciences in Asia*

Social sciences are increasingly gaining recognition and receiving importance in Asia and the Pacific region. From a situation in early 1950s when there was a desperately small number of active social scientists in the region, we have now entered the era of a continuously growing social science enterprise. More and more countries are realizing the need for social sciences in their development programmes, and are thus making demands on the community of social scientists. Social science curricula are being introduced in centres of higher learning, and researches are being undertaken by trained social scientists on problems of national relevance. The social science scene in Asia and the Pacific is rapidly changing.

Growth of Social Sciences in Asia-Pacific Region

Social sciences, as they are currently defined, have arrived in the region from the West. Most Asian cultures, in the pre-colonial phase had traditions of learning which were largely sacred in character, and which emphasized more on the abstract and the abstruse. True, there existed knowledge that had social science relevance but it was not social science. The writings of the time have the tone of prescription and are normative in orientation.

---

* Text of a lecture delivered under the aegis of the Nehru Club, NEHU, Shillong on 11 April, 1990.

The intellectual scene was dominated by thinkers and philosophers, but there were no social scientists, in the modern sense of the term.

The *first* phase of modern social sciences in Asia and the Pacific roughly synchronizes with the first phase of the colonial era. It is characterized by a series of ethnographic studies on the various cultural groups, carried out mainly by the Europeans. First-hand accounts of the Asian cultures based on intensive fieldwork were published by the anthropologists, travellers, missionaries and administrators; this material constitutes the first set of social science literature about this region. However, it is the "queer", the "exotic", the "primitive", and the "eastern-oriental" of these societies which became the subject-matter of the earlier works. Thus, while social sciences were gaining ground in the West as a major intellectual movement, Asian societies became the objects of study for the practitioners of the new discipline. Anthropology, for example, was defined as a study of the "other societies". Social scientists in this region became a synonym for outside observers. Asia and the Pacific, thus, contributed to the growth of social sciences in this phase not through its scholarship, but through providing a field for study.

The influence-flow during that period answered the *single-aperture model*: colonies that were largely insulated from the outside influence opened out through the aperture of colonial rule, getting linked with the colonial master in a vertical relationship. All external influences filtered through that aperture, with the colonial rulers performing the gatekeeping function. Colonial masters brought their own scholars—social scientists among others—to assist them in the understanding of local cultures so that their foothold could be strengthened.

Thus, social sciences in Asia-Pacific region began as "outsider" ("expatriate") studies of "native" cultures and social structures. The *second* phase is characterized by two features: (1) establishment of tertiary level teaching in the social sciences in the colonies, and (2) migration of "natives" to the metropolitan centres for higher studies. The returnee natives, in the *third* phase, joined the expatriate researchers and teachers as junior partners, thus making the social science community stratified among outsiders-insiders. Over the years, more and more insiders have joined the ranks and have succeeded in outnumbering the outsiders. In the post-colonial phase, the insiders in most countries have taken up major responsibilities of teaching and research, and the "outsiders" are pushed to the peripheries. The "outsiders" and the outside influences have also become more diverse: with the attainment of independence the single-aperture model got replaced by a *multiple-aperture model*—having several openings and plurality of entries and exits.

The colonial phases in the history of the Asia-Pacific countries had thus the most decisive influence on the growth of various branches of knowledge, and on the general intellectual climate. With the attainment of independence, the culture of the college became more open. Two things happened: (1) Single-aperture model was replaced by the multiplicity of apertures. (2) The earlier single aperture got somewhat narrowed down—because of the prevalence of an attitude of ambivalence, intellectuals started looking for different reference groups than the colonizer country. The flow of intellectuals from, and to, the newly independent countries became diversified; for different purposes, different apertures became significant. In addition to United Kingdom, France and the Netherlands, people began to look towards Germany, USSR, and USA for intellectual stimulation. In the field of social sciences, the United States of America emerged as a powerful reference group for most countries of the region.

While social sciences are recent arrivals in Asia and the Pacific region, they did not reach all the countries at the same time. The story of their entry, their recognition, and their growth varies from country to country, and from discipline to discipline. In some of the countries the social science enterprise is well-established and is impressive in size; in several others, it is still struggling for its identity and credibility. There are countries in the region, which produce large number of social science graduates and doctoral researches, and have an impressive flow of publications of international standard; and there are also countries where instruction in most of the social science disciplines is imparted only at the undergraduate level—students aspiring to specialize in many of the social science disciplines have no option but to go abroad. Such is the situation in Sri Lanka, Afghanistan, and Nepal. Even in Iran, only two students were registered for Ph.D. in the year 1974. In Sri Lanka, the university does not have a single full-fledged professor in any of the social science departments: all the undergraduate courses are, therefore, run by lecturers. In Afghanistan, the highest degree awarded by Kabul University is that of B.A., and that is regarded as adequate qualification for a faculty appointment. In Nepal, no postgraduate course is offered in sociology, anthropology, or psychology, although some provision is being made to award Ph.Ds. in sociology and anthropology.

Social science subjects emerged as distinct disciplines through different routes in different countries. Thus, the countries which were influenced by the Dutch or the French educational system started with law. The disciplines of sociology and political science were first taught as a paper, or a course, to the law students. This was the situation in Indonesia, Kampuchea, Iran and Afghanistan. In Indonesia, anthropology arrived through linguistics and prehistory. Philosophy mothered psychology in India, Pakistan, Bangladesh and Burma; and sociology came through the gateway of economics in these countries. The new disciplines of public administration, and of international relations, have recently separated from political science; similarly, the discipline of business administration emerged out of commerce, and of management out of psychology.

In several universities of the region, social sciences are still lumped together with other humanities in the general Faculty of Arts. What constitutes social sciences is also defined separately by various countries. However, there appears to be universal agreement about the core disciplines of sociology, political science, social psychology, social anthropology, and economics. In addition to these, following disciplines are also accorded a social science status in some countries: mass communication, social work, journalism, military science, demography, law, criminology, linguistics, philosophy, education, geography, and commerce.

Distinctive Features of Present-day Social Sciences in the Region

The distinctive features of the Asia-Pacific social sciences may be noted:

1. The first and foremost is the fact that social sciences in this region are relatively recent and in many countries they are still struggling for their recognition and identity. The introduction of social sciences came with the colonial experience. The manner in which individual social sciences grew has been determined by the kind of colonial exposure the societies received.
2. Despite relative recency of their arrival, remarkable growth of social sciences in the region has been noted in the past few years. This is evidenced by the number of social science university departments, research institutes, the size of the social science community, and by the greater volume of publications.
3. The present phase of the growth of social sciences in the region is influenced by the twin processes of decolonization and development. The social science community in the

region is trying to introduce the relevance of their work to national development and to re-think how the various theories and methodologies that they have freely borrowed from the outside may be meaningful in their environment. There has been a trend towards replacement of foreign faculty and foreign language as medium of instruction. Moreover, many curbs have been introduced on expatriate research. The new concern for *development* has also influenced significantly the growth of social sciences. There is a new opportunity for social scientists to effectively contribute to the process of national development, social change, and modernization.

4. The demographic profile of the social science community is undergoing rapid change. There *is* now an increasingly high percentage of locally trained social scientists who are young in age. With the new opportunities available, many native scholars have started returning from foreign countries. New programmes of international exchange have also contributed to the mobility of scholars and thus to the process of brain-drain.
5. There is now much demand for social science expertise. It is needed in higher education, in the government, and in business and industry. Even within the university system, there is a demand for social science orientation in professional courses such as agriculture, medicine, and engineering.
6. With the increase in the size of the social science community, and with their increasing recognition, some countries are witnessing a trend towards professionalization of social sciences. There are, for example, discipline-based national associations. In some countries, there are social science councils or academies at the national level to carry out and to promote research. New journals in social sciences have appeared on the scene. There is also a trend towards establishment of research institutes both within and outside the universities.

7. The introduction of computer culture and quantitative techniques in social research requires training in those skills which most of the senior social scientists in less developed countries do not possess, and are thus unable to introduce these in the teaching curricula. This knowledge gap hampers growth of social sciences, and their utilization for purposes of development.
8. The social science picture, however, is not the same in all the countries. While some countries have highly organized and well developed social science agencies, social sciences in other countries are still in their formative stage. The problems of the two sets of countries are, therefore, not necessarily identical. However, such a situation offers an opportunity for developing collaborative arrangements through which supports could be provided to the countries where facilities do not exist by those countries which have highly developed social sciences.
9. It is paradoxical that while social sciences are becoming more visible, and are regarded as directly concerned with national development, they have failed to attract support from the UNDP. Virtually no UNDP country programme in the region has any project for the training of social scientists. Even a small project to promote regional cooperation in social sciences, supported by several governments, and social scientists of the region, did not find favour with UNDP. Among the international organizations, it is only UNESCO which has, through its regular programme, contributed to the growth of the social sciences in the region, and to regional cooperation through the formation of the Association of Asian Social Science Research Councils (AASSREC) and the Asia-Pacific Information Network in Social Sciences (APINESS).

Key Issues in Asian Social Sciences

Social sciences in Asia and the Pacific are experiencing a different sort of crisis compared to the West. In Europe and

North America, the social sciences are a well-established enterprise. They have long overcome the crisis of recognition. They have gone beyond the phase of descriptive empirical inquiries. They have gained increasing autonomy, and in the process, have begun losing financial support from the state. They have found new patrons in the private sector. Social sciences in the West are now engaged in the battle of paradigms, in questions related to new orientations, interdisciplinarity, quantification, internationalization, and in futurology.

In contrast to this, social sciences in Asia and the Pacific are still grappling with the problem of identification and recognition. They are largely dependent upon state support, and mainly concerned with the problems of the present. Little evidence exists of the coinage of indigenous concepts, of the fashioning of new tools and techniques, and of alternative theory construction. The knowledge base is still poor and insufficient, manpower is inadequate and undertrained, and there is continuing imbalance between the intellectual metropolises and the countries of the region. Key issues in Asia-Pacific social sciences may be noted as under:

Need for Indigenization

On the intellectual front, the key crisis in social sciences in Asia relates to their *indigenization.* The native scholarship has begun raising questions regarding the applicability and appropriateness of theories and methodology imported from abroad, and has started almost a campaign for their replacement by "native categories of thought" and indigenous techniques of research. The call for indigenization, however, takes different forms, and lays emphasis on different aspects in different countries. In countries which have recently introduced social sciences, indigenization is merely a plea for the introduction and recognition of social science so that native scholarship can grow and finally make a contribution to the nation building process. There, the substantive issues are not discussed. In some others, indigenization is expressed in terms of a switchover to the national language as medium of instruction and report writing. Curriculum development, with a bias towards national needs, is also an indicator of indigenization. While considerable reaction against the "external" theories and methodology is in evidence, there is, however, very little by way of construction of an indigenous social science. Much of the thinking on this issue is guided by the national perspectives, and one is not sure whether any Asian perspective is likely to emerge. One will have to watch carefully whether indigenization will lead to a retreat to national shells or to an emergence of parochial regional social sciences in place of a universal-global social science.

It must also be said that in the past few years more channels have been opened for the social scientists to act regionally and even internationally. These apertures should guard against any insular tendencies that might develop as part of the process of indigenization.

Collaboration at the Regional Level

Being relatively recent, and a product of interactions with the West, Asian social science exhibits strong dependency on the West and operates on a very weak framework of relationships between the countries of the region. This was aptly summarized by M.S. Gore when he spoke in the inaugural session of the UNESCO Asian Conference on Teaching and Research in Social Sciences, held in India in 1973. He said: "As we begin this exercise we will find that we know so little about each other though, in a geographical sense, all the countries are neighbours and most of them are experiencing generally similar problems. It is a weakness in our scholarship that we know a great deal about countries of the developed world and their problems and so little about ourselves and our neighbours. Besides, whatever we do know about each other's countries we seem to learn from Western scholars... This calls for much more contact and give and take between the institutions of learning in the countries of this region." It is relevant to note that at this conference the decision was taken to form an Association of Asian Social Science Research Councils (AASSREC) which has now 15 country councils as members, and has become an effective regional organization.

Recognition of Social Sciences other than Economics

Social science growth in the region has largely been governed by the availability of jobs. Since most governments needed economists to fill the posts in the ministries of development, and of planning, the discipline of economics was the first to be established in the universities, and was also the major recipient of government funds for research. There is, thus, imbalance in the social science manpower, and efforts are being made to introduce other disciplines, and also to create job opportunities for them. Many countries are developing programmes to upgrade the skills of the social scientists and to provide them with interdisciplinary orientation.

Need for Stronger Database and Improvement of Techniques of Analysis

Social science data is often inadequate, antiquated, badly collected, and scattered. The same is true about documentation. The need in most countries is that of establishing a centralized social science documentation centre and a data archives, with facilities for electronic data processing and recycling. This is a major infrastructural requirement. Along with it is the need to train documentalists and data archival specialists. Training in the use of computers is also badly needed. Publication of research reports and papers is yet another area which deserves priority action. UNESCO's action to create APINESS—Asia-Pacific Information Network in Social Sciences—is a useful first step in this direction.

Funding

In most countries of the region, government is the major, if not the sole, provider of funds for all social science research. Quite naturally, funds thus made available limit the choice of themes for research. While grants are given for policy-related research projects money is generally not available for theoretical work, or for research in an area that may not be regarded as relevant by the fund-givers. Funds are also made available by some international agencies, and some private foundations of developed countries, such as USA, Canada, UK and Germany. But there are significant contrasts in the level of funding by the two sets of agencies. It is quite often complained that generous grants given by the external agencies spoil the market and wean away good researchers from the national scene. The motivation to do nationally relevant research with funds provided by the national funding agencies is very little; moreover, lack of coördination between funding agencies often results in needless, and avoidable, duplication of effort.

Utilization of Social Sciences

There is a general feeling that social sciences are not being adequately utilized in public policy, and in national development. Much of this complaint relates to the *non-utilization* of research findings, and to the relative *non-involvement* of social scientists. Those against whom this complaint is lodged give their own reasons for non-utilization, or provide evidence of the use they are making. They hint at the non-utilization, of research—in terms both of its relevance and intelligibility, and also specify the exacting demands of administration—speed and efficiency, and political appeal—which go contrary to the equally exacting demands of social science—systematic and careful data gathering, evaluation, criticism, and value-neutrality. The absence of dialogue between the social scientists and policy makers and administrators hampers utilization of available social science knowledge and further generation of relevant knowledge.

Commercialization of the Social Sciences

A natural outgrowth of professionalization of a discipline is its commercialization. Consultancy services offered by some social scientists—particularly psychologists—are regarded by some as an ethically dangerous development. People have begun selling social science advice at unbelievably high prices, and have become, in the process, servants of the industry rather than of the society. Some of the practitioners regard the over-concern with involvement in policy and government programmes also as a part of the commercialization process. Social science capability, according to them, lies not only in listening to the loud voices of the government but in interpreting the unspoken, silent voices of the people. They advocate the need to get rid of excessive dependence on the government—which verges on professional parasitism—and to do solid research without getting manipulated by the authorities.

Some are unhappy with the present patterns of division of labour in the international social science scene where theorizing is done by social scientists of the West and Asian social scientists are content with applied and action research, and that too of a mere descriptive variety. It is argued by them that social sciences should not only be an instrument of the modern state but should also attempt a critical analysis of policies. Rather than simply supporting a programme for the demolition of traditional-cultural values, social scientists must examine their relevance in the context of change and development, and may even suggest their preservation and utilization in nation building and development.

Social Sciences in the 1990s

Having briefly reviewed the internal crises of the social sciences which would demand efforts in the coming years, let us now see what the social sciences as they stand today on the thresholds of the 1990s are expected to do for the society.

Social sciences are expected to provide valid diagnoses of the world problems of the day and to identify the emerging trends so that appropriate measures can be taken before the trends get transformed into the crises. The one world we live in is characterized by regional specificities and cultural diversities. There are concerns for development that the entire world shares; there are problems that the entire world confronts. But the concerns assume regional and local colour, and the global problems present different parochial profiles. It is desirable to recognize this fact and evolve suitable strategies to meet the challenges of the times so that each region receives adequate attention and each problem is resolved in accordance with the situational context in which it occurs. Resolution of problems requires an interdisciplinary approach, that keeps man at the centre, and focuses emphatically on the utilization and application of knowledge. In the Asia-Pacific region the need for applied and action research is the greatest, and the problem of the non-utilization of research findings is the gravest. Effort is needed both to promote applied research and to establish channels of communication between producers and consumers of research.

The concept of *problem* also needs to be properly defined. In this context, it is necessary to distinguish between (1) problems that are regarded as "pathological" and require a clinical approach, and (2) problems that are "developmental" based on the philosophy of the "desirable" requiring action for the creation of a better future. It must be said that the existing paradigm of development, with a heavy emphasis on exogenous source of influence and aid, described several situations in the countries of the Asia-Pacific region as problems of the first order and adopted a "clinical" and sectoral approach to deal with them. It is time to recognize that the various problems constitute a complicated pattern of interrelationships and they are intertwined in circular cause-effect linkages. This means that a system of priorities will have to be carefully thought through.

Rather than assigning ranks in a scale of priorities, it will perhaps be advisable, to view each problem in relation to other problems and to work out the range of its ramifications.

Problems may also be classified in terms of a time frame: those that deserve immediate attention, and those that require "anticipatory" action in a long-term perspective. Analysis of the past two development decades indicates that sectoral approach in handling individual problems has created several imbalances. For instance, exclusive emphasis on economic growth, to the almost total neglect of the "human factor", has had grave consequences. Thus, while average incomes have doubled, they have widened the gaps between the rich and the poor because of lack of a policy of social justice. Programmes of health and family planning have helped both in the reduction of death and birth rates but the change in demographic pyramid brought about by these changes has not been properly taken into account in formulating developmental policies. Increasing infant and young population has created demands for the education system and the job market, which are hardly met; rise in literacy and education has transformed the profile of the "unemployed"—the size of the "educated unemployed" and their aspirations for the urban jobs demand a better "fit" between education and employment. The wild race for industrialization through external aid has created newer sets of dependencies; and these are further complicated by the "sudden" energy crisis which futurologists had earlier failed to forecast.

The Asia-Pacific region is a home of more than half of the world's total population. It is marked by topographic and climatic extremes and a great diversity of cultures, social structures, and political systems. It is estimated that in about 10 years time, this region will have as many people as the entire world had in the year 1950. What was regarded as global scale once will become "regional" in the years to come.

Several features are distinctive of this region:

1. Despite slowing down of the global population growth rate, the region continues to have higher rates compared to the developed world. As a result, a major share in world population will be contributed by the region. In absolute numbers, the figures will be astounding. To quote *Asia 1989 Yearbook*: "By the end of this century both China and India will have populations in excess of a billion and four Asian countries–Bangladesh, Indonesia, Japan and Pakistan– will have populations numbering in excess of 100 million."
2. Because of the success of programmes of health and education, two things have happened in Asia. The mortality rate has sharply declined and the number of educated among the younger population has risen. The new demography of Asia reveals an increasing percentage of both the aging population and the younger age groups, necessitating emphasis on programmes of training and employment for the youth and programmes of social welfare for the aged.
3. Vast masses of Asia's population are still in the rural areas. Because of the *urban bias* in development there has been neglect of the rural areas which are also the pockets of absolute poverty. According to a World Bank report, "Half of the people in absolute poverty live in South Asia, mainly in India and Bangladesh. A sixth live in East and Southeast Asia, mainly in Indonesia... (The) poor are primarily rural dwellers, overwhelmingly dependent on agriculture–the majority of them being landless."
4. A majority of the countries of this region got their independence–from the colonial rulers–in the past 40-45 years. The post-independence era was characterized by the twin processes of decolonization and development. Recent reviews of the nation building exercises reveal that the countries are still tied by dependency relationships creating inequities and imbalances and hampering endogenous development, including indigenization of knowledge.

Internally also, the gaps between the elite and the masses have widened and national integration has not been achieved because of political instability, weak infrastructures, communal violence, infringement of human rights, and slow economic growth associated with maldistribution of income.

5. Countries of this region suffer from several types of natural disasters. Earthquakes, floods, typhoons, and cyclones have recurred in several countries of the region—China, Pakistan, India, the Philippines, Indonesia, and Burma. These disasters have both technological and human dimensions, and they invite immediate attention involving a fire-fighting approach.

   In this region, the refugee influx has largely been caused by political events in Kampuchea, Vietnam, and in Afghanistan.

6. Another distinctive feature of this region is the new phenomenon of international migration. This has two aspects: increase in tourism, and migration of skilled and unskilled labour to oil-rich countries of the Middle East. Both these features affect not only the economy of the countries receiving tourists and exporting labour, they also make several "adjustments" necessary and create a variety of problems in the process.

In evolving an agenda for social sciences in the region it will be advisable to keep the above features in mind. It must be stressed that the problems that the region faces are not radically different from those faced by other regions of the world, nor has the syndrome of problems changed over the years; if at all, there is an aggravation of problems, and a differentiation of their manifestation in various member-states. Attempts at the resolution of the problems have led to several changes, the ramifications of which have added more disturbing features.

In the countries of the Third World, to which the Asia-Pacific region belongs, action is needed to resolve problems that confront them today and now. This requires a major investment in research. Social structures and cultures of many of these countries are undergoing radical transformations; such a situation not only offers excellent opportunity for the investigation of the processes of change, but also requires urgent attention to record the existing patterns before they disappear as a result of directed cultural change. There is an urgent need to carry out studies of values, institutions, social structure, traditional technology, and worldview to document the rich cultural heritage of man. No doubt, anthropological studies carried out by expatriates provide good records of these societies, but these are "outside" views and have become dated; moreover, they are microcosmic accounts.

It must be stressed that the countries of the Asia-Pacific region do not constitute a homogeneous whole. They are at different stages of development and they differ in terms of available scientific manpower, know-how, and technology. Emphasis in priorities may differ in different sets of countries: the LDCs, the countries of the ASEAN region, the Indo-Chinese countries, South-Asian countries, Pacific countries, and developed countries (like Australia, Japan, and New Zealand).

It is also desirable to identify specific problems for certain key population groups: women, youth, refugees, ethnic minorities, disabled, and the aged. It must, however, be said that these categories are not mutually exclusive; far example, the category of women will include young, aged, disabled refugees, and the ethnic minorities. So will be true of the youth.

The overview of social science situation attempted in this paper suggests that action is needed on two fronts:

Development and Strengthening of Academic Infrastructures

This would involve setting up or reinforcing institutions of learning and research, promotion of basic research, building up of trained cadres of researchers, teachers, and development personnel; and promotion of regional and international cooperation and collaboration.

Initiating Programmes of Research on Priority Problems in all Spheres of Societal Life

Social scientists in the region are expected to perform the dual role of being *analysts* of change, and *agents* to change. Not only are they prescribing the tasks that they ought to perform, other sectors of the national and international community are also making demands on them. In such a situation, it is difficult to arrive at a consensus view regarding the role of the social scientist, or even the priorities of research. Since the problems are too many—both social and academic—it is expected that different scholars will choose their own menu and contribute to the social science cuisine. Action on any of the priority areas would be welcome provided it is based on competence, plurality of approaches, critical analysis, and comparative perspective.

There is so much to be done that the coming decades will be of virtual no-holiday for the social sciences. If the previous decades laid emphasis on economic growth, education, and science and technology, the coming decades are likely to seek help from social sciences to assess the past performance, analyze the present crises, and to develop blueprints for the future. This is neither possible with the existing manpower nor with the available stock of knowledge. We are called upon not only to disseminate existing knowledge and ensure its utilization but, more importantly, to engage in the *generation* of new knowledge and ideas.

2

Growth Points in Asian and Pacific Sociology and Social Anthropology*

The vast Asia-Pacific region, with a multitude of societies and a variety of cultures, has a sociological treasure house and an anthropological gold mine. The old civilizations of this region have nourished indigenous traditions of social thought and social philosophy. Western scholarship found this zone a virgin territory for explorations and for building up a theoretical edifice for the understanding of society.

Sociological and social anthropological literature is replete with material drawn from the societies of the region. And yet little is known about the status of the twin disciplines of sociology and social anthropology as they have developed here. In terms of research, this is a well covered territory; in terms of teaching, in the region's universities, the two disciplines are a relatively recent arrival even compared with some other social science disciplines. In other words, while there is an impressive bibliography of sociology and anthropology of Asia and the Pacific, Asian and Pacific sociology and anthropology are still in their formative stage.

---

* Reprinted from *Sociology and Social Anthropology in Asia and the Pacific* (ed. Yogesh Atal), Wiley Eastern Ltd., New Delhi, 1985, Chapter 1.

The essays contained in this volume provide, for the first time, an opportunity to study the growth of these disciplines in the region. This chapter draws on these essays and some other available material in presenting a regional profile of sociology and social anthropology.

The Beginnings

As subject matter for study by ethnographers and social anthropologists, the societies and cultures of this region have been the field of much research activity ever since they came in contact with the West. Numerous travellers, traders, missionaries, and colonial administrators have contributed considerable material in the form of diaries, travelogues, essays, and memoranda about the "queer" and "exotic" peoples and their customs. Though these highly personalized and mostly biased accounts are not entirely dependable, they provided data for systematization by armchair scholars in the West and paved the way for the emergence of social and cultural anthropology in Western academia. Later, Asia and the Pacific region, as also the continent of Africa, served as the training ground and research site for the Western anthropologists. It is worth noting that first generation of social anthropologists and sociologists of the region received their training in the West; they learned theory and methodology in the Western universities but did field work in their own countries. With this, social anthropology ceased to be the study only of "other cultures".

To recapitulate: modern social science arrived in the region from the West; first researches in these societies were conducted by Western scholars, the first departments of sociology and social anthropology were manned by them, and the first students from the region were trained mostly in the West. Sociology and social anthropology in the contemporary sense are indeed a Western implantation.

The arrival of these disciplines in the region is associated with the process of colonization. Thus sociology and social anthropology in South Asia (India, Bangladesh, Pakistan, Sri Lanka), in Malaysia and Singapore, in Australia and New Zealand bear the imprint of the British tradition; Indonesia has Dutch influence; and the Philippines clearly reflect an American orientation. Similarly, the Koreans speak of the influence of Japanese colonization on their intellectual style. Even the societies that were not politically colonized have gone through a process of vicarious colonization in academic fields. Sociology in China, for example, started under the powerful influence of the works of Herbert Spencer; Thailand borrowed its orientation both from the British and the American universities; Japan has similarly been influenced by German, British, and American intellectual traditions.

In many ways, the Australian and New Zealand situation is identical to that obtaining in the United States. These two countries, being societies of immigrants, encouraged their scholars to study the native aboriginal populations. Within their own newly acquired homeland they found an excellent opportunity to study "other cultures"—the subject matter for anthropological study. Being descendants of Europeans, the Australian and New Zealand sociologists and social anthropologists have no difficulty in relating themselves to the ethos of the Western civilization; unlike Americans, they have, however, not yet fashioned a distinctive style of their own. In many ways, their educational system is an extension of the British system. Their intellectual dependence on the home country is characteristic of them; some of their more eminent scholars moved to the metropolitan centre, for example, Raymond Firth. This is also reflected in the relative recency of the introduction of sociology into universities in Australia and New Zealand as is true in Britain. Some other countries of the region have a fairly long history of teaching of sociology.

It is important to mention that opposition to the introduction of sociology in university curricula in Australia and in New Zealand came mostly from the professors with an

Oxbridge orientation. And this is understandable; after all, Oxford does not have a department of sociology even now, and the Cambridge chair in sociology was established as late as 1968. It is only the so-called "redbrick" universities in the United Kingdom which have teaching departments of sociology. It is common knowledge that social sciences, leaving aside anthropology, "were not part of the old English academic tradition and by implication, therefore, they were of no consequence." Way back in 1955, Partridge in his essay on "Research in the Social Sciences at Australian Universities" (published in *International Social Science Bulletin,* Vol. 7, No. 1) wrote that there were

> ...many...[who] are not convinced that there is any separate discipline of sociology; they argue that all the important problems dealt with by sociologists can be more minutely and rigorously studied by one or other of the existing social sciences.

New Zealand also faced similar opposition. While the University of New Zealand has conducted examinations in introductory sociology since the 1920s, it did not offer any formal teaching. So great was the opposition to social sciences in New Zealand that one of its Prime Ministers—W.F. Massey—has gone on record to say in 1922 that "if he had his way he would burn the whole damned lot of their useless publications" (Craig, 1964: 197). Another Prime Minister—Peter Fraser—was even opposed to the introduction of a course in "social work". He thought that permitting training in social work would "imply an admission that governmental social welfare policies had been inadequate". He, however, agreed to the naming of the department as "School of Social Sciences" in place of Social Work.[1] It was at this school that in 1957 a year long introductory course in sociology for B.A. students was first introduced in New Zealand. Courses at M.A. level were available in this country only from 1965 when Canterbury University at Christchurch launched its programme of postgraduate studies. Victoria University at Wellington followed suit in 1967. Subsequently, courses in sociology were started at Waikato, Auckland, and Massey universities. Only Otago University—which has the oldest department of anthropology, started in 1919—does not have a course in sociology.

In Australia, sociology was promoted by A.P. Elkin, who succeeded Raymond Firth in 1933 as professor of anthropology at the University of Sydney. Following a lead from A.R. Radcliffe-Brown, Elkin introduced a course in comparative sociology; but he attributed a different meaning to the term. Unlike Radcliffe-Brown, who was interested in the comparative method for the establishment of universal laws, Elkin "encouraged his students to seek answers to specific and practical problems of their own society (such as migrant assimilation, post-war reconstruction, social consequences of industrialization, etc.)." It is important, however, to mention that the first university chair in sociology was established at the University of New South Wales in the year 1958; although, as part of philosophy, the subject has been taught at Sydney since 1909, and at Melbourne since 1919. It was in the 1960s that five departments of sociology were established in Australia. Today, all the nineteen universities offer some courses in sociology. As against this only six universities have chairs in anthropology but there are only two separate departments, others are combined with sociology (2 cases) and with psychology (1) and prehistory (1).

The academic culture in the Indian subcontinent shares some traits with the Australia-New Zealand system of higher education in that both are products of British influence and imposition. The major difference in the two situations is the existence of an ancient, powerful and live indigenous civilization in the Indian subcontinent made up of many "little" traditions fusing into several "great" traditions. The complexity of Indian culture posed problems not only for the colonial administration but also opened great and challenging opportunities for alien scholarship. The rudimentary beginnings of social anthropology and sociology in the Indian subcontinent can be attributed to this initial encounter. Long before a system of modern education was set up on the subcontinent and these disciplines received recognition, a spate of publications appeared on the tribes and castes of India written by colonial administrators and Christian missionaries. The district gazetteers and census monographs can be regarded as exercises in social anthropology by the colonial administration. They were a definite aid to administration. To quote the author of the chapter on India :

> ....the colonial administration found sociology and social anthropology to be useful instruments of colonial domination. Thus, the indispensability of the knowledge of Indian society for smooth administration created much of the impetus for sociology and social anthropology.
>
> Francis Buchanan's famous travelogues written in the early 19th century, B.H. Baden Powell's pioneering work on *Land Systems of British India*, Risley's *The Peoples of India*, studies on castes and tribes by Nesfield, W.Crook, E.Thurston, and J.H. Hutton, work on the village communities by Henry Maine and Baden Powell, Grierson's monumental *Linguistic Survey of India*, all these were inspired by the same urge for basic data and information that the colonial administration required for effective functioning (p. 315).

Prior to independence from the British and partition of the country, the three present-day countries of the subcontinent—India, Pakistan, and Bangladesh—went through a common colonial experience under the same regime. In the country's two prestigious universities—Calcutta and Bombay—the British introduced these subjects in the early part of the twentieth century. The School of Economics and Sociology was created in Bombay University under the leadership of Sir

Patrick Geddes in 1914, and a department of anthropology was set up at Calcutta University in 1917. Besides, the government also set up a separate Anthropological Survey of India; its headquarters were first located in Benares (now called Varanasi) and then transferred to Calcutta. In other universities, these subjects started their journey as part of the syllabi in economics, philosophy, or political science. In south India, Mysore University took the lead in introducing sociology papers in philosophy in the 1930s. Madras Museum hired Aiyappan—a student of Raymond Firth—to develop an anthropological wing almost at the same time. At a much later date, in the late 1940s, the University of Lucknow introduced these subjects in the department of economics, where the first teachers in sociology were those trained in economics—even those majoring in sociology received their degrees initially in economics. Teaching in anthropology, however, was started by D.N. Majumdar, who was recruited first as a lecturer in primitive economics. It is quite significant that the old and established universities have generally been reticent in introducing these disciplines—a pattern similar to the Australian and New Zealand situation. Thus, while the newly established universities in India (a functional equivalent of the redbrick universities) were hospitable to the introduction of these subjects, the old universities resisted. For example, while Delhi University had a department of anthropology (mostly devoted to physical anthropology and prehistory) its sociology department came into being in 1958. Departments of sociology in the Banaras Hindu University and the Aligarh Muslim University were set up much later. Madras University has only recently started teaching sociology. Even Punjab University started sociology in 1959-1960. Calcutta University created a chair in sociology, but it remained vacant for a number of years; it was only in the late 70s that teaching in sociology was started there.

The same is true of Pakistan and Bangladesh. For example, in Pakistan the teaching of sociology at the Punjab University in Lahore was started in 1950 as an optional paper in economics, political science, history, and philosophy. It was only in 1955 that the Punjab University in Lahore started its M.A. course in sociology. While sociology, or more precisely rural sociology, is now taught in some other universities in Pakistan, the teaching of anthropology has recently been introduced in the newly set up Qaid-e-Azam University in Islamabad. In what is now Bangladesh, sociology and social anthropology did not find an independent place until 1950. Before independence (i.e. 1947), Dacca University (established in 1921) worked in unison with Calcutta University where the students from this part of the subcontinent received training in anthropology. At Dacca University, sociology was taught as a part of the syllabus for political economy and political science. It was at the initiative of the famous French anthropologist Levi-Strauss, who went to Dacca as a UNESCO consultant, that Dacca University established a separate department of sociology, which started functioning in 1957. Now sociology is also taught at Rajshahi and Chittagong universities, and at the Bangladesh Agricultural University in Mymensingh.

Taking the three countries—India, Pakistan, Bangladesh—together, one finds a fairly long tradition of teaching and research in the two disciplines. For example, Bombay University's department of sociology celebrated its golden jubilee in 1969. However, treated separately in both Pakistan and in Bangladesh these disciplines were introduced in the 1950s; while there is only one department of anthropology in Pakistan, in Bangladesh there is none, although sociology at Dacca has a bias towards social anthropology.

British administrators and anthropologists studied the culture and society in the Indian subcontinent; the Dutch made initial contributions towards the understanding of Indonesian society. The Dutch writers not only tried to describe the various ethnic communities and cultures of the vast archipelago but also attempted to cast data in the then prevalent theoretical moulds. Thus, G.A. Wilken employed an evolutionary framework; J.H. Boeke came up with his formulation of a dualistic economy; and W.H. Rassers utilized the diffusion theory to explain similarities in mythological themes. A number of writers dwelt on the customary law (*adat)*. Most of these studies were described as a part of "Indologie" (study of the peoples and cultures of the Indies) and were carried out by people belonging to various disciplinary backgrounds. Such a "wide scope of *Taal-Land-en Volkenkunde*[2] and *Indologie* became the original area of contact from which various social science disciplines branched off" in Indonesia. In this country, law and history promoted research in anthropology and sociology. It is interesting to note that the first Indonesian occupant of the sociology chair—G.T.S. Mulia—was a social philosopher and his successor—Ismael—a social geographer. The first institution for higher education in social sciences in Indonesia was set up in 1924. The Law College of Batavia (now Jakarta) provided a four-year course in law with emphasis on *adat* law. In addition to teaching courses in law, the college also offered introductory courses in economics, sociology and anthropology. Universities came into being in the wake of independence. After independence, a number of students went to American universities—mainly Cornell, M.I.T., and Yale—for training in sociology and social anthropology. These foreign trained scholars now occupy important positions in the Indonesian universities.

The Philippines experienced two colonizations. Way back in the 16th and 17th centuries the Spanish colonizers brought anthropology to this archipelago; with the second colonization in 1898, by the Americans, the tradition of anthropological writing about the indigenous peoples received further impetus. As with the British and the Dutch, both the colonizers of this country resorted to anthropology to meet their need to know local customs and practices, to incorporate tribal segments into the "mainstream" Philippine society, to satisfy their curiosity about exotic cultures, and to promote protestant evangelization. Thus, anthropology in the Philippines "started as a practical activity of men in the service of religion and government". To this end, an "Ethnological Survey of the Philippines" was set up in 1903. Teaching of ethnology was started within the department of history in 1914, and later it was granted the status of a separate department in 1917 only to be merged again in 1921 with the newly created department of sociology. Notwithstanding such a long duration, the then professor of anthropology at the university—Dr Beyer—"trained only two MAs in 40 years"! The tradition of teaching of sociology also goes as far back as 1896 when it was taught as a part of social philosophy. Later, it became a problem and/or welfare oriented discipline. It was only after the Second World War that sociology began to be taught as a scientific study of society. American interest in these disciplines continued in the post-war period, but the Americans had a very specific focus: they attempted "to understand factors and processes involved in the integration of the Philippines into a nation state and the role of the American administrators in helping to bring it about".

In Philippine social anthropology and sociology the American influence has been the strongest. Whatever British influence reached the Philippines, did so via that route. The academic metropolis for the Filipino social anthropologists has been the Chicago school under the leadership of Fred Eggan[2]. Since A.R. Radcliffe-Brown—the proponent of British structural-functional school and a mentor of Eggan—was at Chicago, the Filipino anthropologists being trained there received and imbibed elements of British orientation as well.

We may now turn to the situation in Japan and the Republic of Korea. Japanese sociology was influenced by the writings of the scholars belonging to the European "formal" school—Simmel, Vierkandt and von Wiese. But very little sociological work was done before and during the Second

World War, barring some notable contributions to Japanese family system and rural social structure by Teizo Toda, Eitaro Suzuke, and Kizaemon Aruga. After the war, sociologists interested themselves in the study of social change. Work in the area of urban sociology was initiated by Fukutaro Okui and Elichi Isomura. "The efforts of Japanese sociologists proceeded in two directions. One was to introduce sociological theory and thought through translations and interpretations of mainly American works. The other was to apply American methods to field studies. The former led to the diversification of Japanese sociology into many subfields; the latter led to a survey boom" (Koyano, 1974: 347). By 1966, only 26 of the 345 universities (national, public, and private) had graduate schools of sociology. However, sociology courses were offered in liberal arts in as many as 150 universities. In a survey conducted by Koyano it emerged that the older generation of sociologists have a greater liking for European scholars compared with the younger ones who prefer American sociologists. But in both the groups Talcott Parsons and Robert Merton are very highly regarded. Such an orientation of sociologists accounts for a complete separation between sociology and social anthropology in Japan. It should also be mentioned that Japanese sociology is divided into two distinct camps: Marxist and non-Marxist. This division came to the surface in the 1950s when the younger generation of sociologists started critically reviewing American influenced sociology.

In the Republic of Korea, although Korean words for anthropology, social contract, evolution, social organization figured in publications of the late 1890s, sociology was still a relatively unknown discipline until 1910 when the country was annexed to Japan. It is through the Japanese and Chinese translations of Western works in the fields of anthropology and sociology that the first generation of sociologists and anthropologists was trained. It must be said, however, that during the Japanese occupation (1910-1945) not much academic activity in the field of the social sciences was encouraged for obvious political reasons.

The disciplines of sociology and anthropology received greater impetus from scholars of the Republic of Korea who returned after their training in Europe and the United States. They wrote books introducing the subject matter of sociology and the main trends in sociology thought. Although Japanese influence on Korean sociological is acknowledged, little is known about the courses taught during the Japanese occupation. Early teaching in sociology is said to have been started by an American missionary in 1981. In 1926, a Japanese sociologist—Takashi Akiba—joined the Keijo Imperial University (which later became Seoul National University) to teach sociology in the department of philosophy. He not only taught sociology but also initiated anthropological fieldwork in Korea. It is important to note that while a good deal of anthropological fieldwork was carried out, the subject was not included in the university curricula until 1945. As author of the chapter on the Republic of Korea puts it: "The sociological interest lay more in importing and disseminating what was then known to have been a new social science developing in the West, whereas the anthropological emphasis was in doing fieldwork to find out about Korean society. No doubt, both disciplines suffered from the colonial experience: suppression of sociology and cooptation of anthropology" (see pp. 92-93). When an independent department of sociology was set up in the Seoul National University in 1946 it was manned by two Koreans trained in Waseda (Japan). Anthropology, though it existed for some time as a separate department, never functioned because there was no staff; the sociology department, however, did offer some courses in anthropology. The author of the chapter on the Republic of Korea regards the return of these two sociologists after their training in the United States (at Cornell and North Carolina respectively) as a landmark: "This event came to be the beginning of direct importation of American sociology to the soil of Korean sociology which required rather a new breed of science after a decade of a diet of rehash of western sociology through earlier Japanese education. This was to be followed by an increased flow of sociology students to United States... For anthropology as well, Hae Young Lee not only began to offer courses... but he also edited the very first introductory textbook in 1958" (pp. 94-95).

The situation in Thailand with regard to sociology and social anthropology provides a good illustration of the vicarious colonization of the academic world by the West. These disciplines came as part of the package of Western education introduced by the indigenous rulers. As everywhere, Thailand also attracted Westerners interested in studying oriental cultures. Earlier writings were in the form of travellers' accounts. These were followed by community studies, ethnographic descriptions of the royal court, and description of the way of life of the hill people. No Thai was formally trained in these disciplines until 1960. Anthropological research teams from American universities opened a new era. The author of the chapter on Thailand reports: "The 1960s mark the golden decade for Americans specializing in Thai studies. This was the period when research funds were abundant and anthropological research projects were being supported both by the American Government and private funding agencies. It is undeniable that the Vietnam war had had its impact on the development of anthropological studies in Thailand." It should also be noted that besides Americans, anthropologists from the United Kingdom, Australia, the Netherlands, Germany, and Japan have also contributed a good deal to the growth of sociological and anthropological studies in Thailand. The introduction of sociology in teaching dates back to 1940 when it was taught in the School of Public Administration. But in the university it was first introduced in 1950 at the Chulalongkorn University in the faculty of political science. It was given the status of a separate specialization in 1964. Later a joint department of sociology and anthropology was set up at Thammasat University. The faculty member were initially sent for further training to the United States (Cornell, California, Chicago, Kansas) and to the United Kingdom (Oxford and the School of Oriental and African Studies), and their orientations are reflected in the structure of courses offered at the leading universities in Thailand.

The peculiar socio-cultural context and the specific historical factors of each of these countries determined the course of sociology and anthropology in the region. This broad survey clearly reveals that the societies of the East have served as sites for much anthropological research and writing. But all of this early literature represents an "outside view". The researchers approached these as "other cultures", and the motivations to visit these cultures and to report on them have been varied, though the predominant concern was a part of the colonization syndrome. In terms of research, anthropology has a longer history than sociology. The teaching of sociology in the region is comparatively recent. Leaving aside introductory courses in sociology offered in other faculties, it can be confidently stated that recognition of sociology and anthropology as academic specialities occurred in the Second World War period. It is also striking that the newly established universities have included the teaching of sociology and social anthropology more often than old universities. It is interesting that while there are more researchers and researches in the field of anthropology, there are fewer departments of anthropology than sociology, and that people trained in anthropology have been instrumental in setting up departments of sociology. With the creation of university departments in these two disciplines and availability of indigenous scholars, trained in them, the relationship between these disciplines has assumed a new dimension. We will discuss this debate in the section that follows.

Sociology and social anthropology in Asia and the Pacific have entered a new phase. Although at different stages of development in different countries, these two disciplines share a common feature. No longer are the societies of this region a mere subject matter for study by expatriate scholarship alone. Indigenous scholars have begun researching their own societies. The scholars are also called upon by their national governments to participate in the process of development and provide expert assistance. Anthropology and sociology, in the newer context, are not to serve the cause of the colonial masters; they are expected to serve the national interests. This has necessitated a new identification of priorities for research. The confrontation is not so much between sociology and anthropology as between native and alien scholarship. It is this new concern that has raised the demand for the indigenization of the social sciences.

Relation between Sociology and Social Anthropology

A glimpse into the history of the growth of these two disciplines in the Asia and Pacific region tells us also about the nature of the relationship between them. Instances are found where the two disciplines exist as separate specialities, and also where the two are merged either as joint departments (department of sociology and anthropology) or as departments with one name but incorporating both the disciplines. Since anthropology was the first to arrive, many sociology departments were set up by social anthropologists. Of course, there are also instances where the two disciplines came via different routes but got merged.

The *raison d'être* of the two disciplines is to be found in the Western intellectual tradition where sociology developed as a study of Western society as against anthropology which was devoted to the study of "other cultures"—variously called primitive, non-literate, small, traditional, and autochthonous. This division of labour between the two specialties is further sharpened by the use of different methods—intensive, long-duration participant observation in case of anthropological investigation, and survey methods in case of sociological studies. The original unified discipline of anthropology was defined as "the study of Man at all levels of cultural development", as "a mirror for Man", as a study of "Man and His Works". Such a broad definition of the discipline of anthropology required its students to receive training in prehistoric archaeology, paleontology, primatology, physical anthropology, ethnology, and linguistics. As a unifying science of Man, the ambitious anthropology of the past had an interdisciplinary orientation. Its claims for a total science of Man notwithstanding, the discipline somehow focussed only on the primitive and the past or talked about our "primitive contemporaries".

The present-day anthropologists are more modest in their claims. So says Maurice Freedman :

> If anthropology were the study of Society and societies and of Culture and cultures, without qualification, it would be grotesquely encyclopedic, and no men could be found to practice it. Even to suggest that it might tend towards realizing so englobing a plan would be to raise the flag of an intolerable scholastic imperialism... Social and cultural anthropology is for the vast majority of its adherents a practicable subject because it is limited in scope—although few, if any scholars can practise all of it .... In recent times it has been common enough for anthropologists to class themselves as specialists in (some would say, sociologists of) primitive society, that form of society being in turn defined as non-literate, small in scale, and based upon a simple technology. (Some would add a further criterion: absence of money.) (Freedman, 1978: 8-9).

With increasing specialization of the various branches within the discipline of anthropology, one finds physical anthropology getting closer to biological sciences and social anthropology to social sciences. It is not without significance that social and cultural anthropologists also use words such as "comparative sociology", or "sociology of primitive society", or even "*Niet-Westersche Sociologie*" (sociology of non-western societies).

Some other factors promoting a closer identification of social anthropology with sociology may also be noted.

Anthropological research evidence has brought out the fact that primitive societies are not always "microcosms" or "homogeneous" entities. There are wide variations: "some indeed are very small, others large; some lack centralized forms of government, others have state forms; some have very simple technologies, others quite complicated ones" (Freedman, 1978: 10). Many of these societies have acquired writing and thus have become literate. The process of transformation and modernization initiated by the colonial rule resulted in the breakdown of insulations and the creation of communicating linkages between the tribals and the neighbouring rural and urban communities. Finding the traditional method of fieldwork applicable to the small village communities, the anthropologists have extended their scope of investigation and moved into the domain that once belonged exclusively to rural sociologists.

Recent decades have also witnessed the arrival of specialists from social science disciplines other than social anthropology into the tribal areas and "other" non-Western societies for purpose of research. Thus, these societies no longer remain a monopoly of the anthropologists.

The training of the so-called "natives" in anthropology has added a new feature. Although students from Asia and the Pacific went in the initial phase to the Western universities for specialization in anthropology, they were sent by those centres back to their own cultures for fieldwork on the basis of which they wrote their dissertations. By doing this, the Western leaders of the profession violated the very definition of the discipline that they had themselves fashioned. One would hesitate to impute motives, but the consequence of such a trend was clear. The new genre of students drawn from the colonies studied their own societies; although these were "other cultures" and "non-Western" for the Western professorate, they were not so for the Asian students.

It must, however, be said that one of the reasons that confined Asians to the study of their own societies is the non-availability of resources for studying other societies. Resources permitting, some of them would perhaps wish to study those societies which produced the early anthropologists and thus justify the traditional definition of the discipline.

There is another compelling reason, however, for the Asian students to study their own societies. Earlier studies were viewed by them not only as biased but also full of gaps; furthermore, the passage of time has made them dated. They feel the necessity to correct the image, to restudy and update them, to investigate many of the unexplored areas and themes, and also document the process of directed culture change initiated by the governments in the post-independence era. The rapidity of change has created a need to study existing reality before it is drastically transformed. Despite the devotion of Western anthropologists to the study of cultures of this region, they could not cover all the ethnic groups. With the availability of native scholarship trained in the discipline the possibility of total coverage has increased. Problems of resource constraint, language difficulty, and establishing rapport are not so acute for the native anthropologists.

The argument that methodological problems involved in the study of other societies are vastly different and it is these that give anthropology a distinction can no longer be sustained in the new circumstances. The anthropologists and their "objects" did not remain in these cases "mutually exotic". A distinction based on the nationality of the investigator rather than the subject matter of study cannot justify the existence of two disciplines; nor can any particular method of investigation be treated as a monopoly of a given discipline. It would be absurd to call a study done by a native and by an outsider on the same theme sociology in one case and anthropology in the other.

For example, to regard a work on caste by the British author J.H. Hutton as anthropology and by the Indian author G.S. Ghurye as sociology makes a mockery of the whole distinction. But the promoters of this outside-inside distinction have not given up their battle. Freedman argues that the "distancing between the observer and the observed in the 'classical' mode of field study is upto a point reproduced in the relationship between the 'new' anthropologists and the people he studies, even though he and they are members of one society; Africa, India, and some countries in Latin America provide very good examples because of their ethnic heterogeneity. Moreover, social scientists are not peasants or workers and are rarely drawn from their ranks. Indeed, it is probably the case that the bourgeois or member of the elite often sees in anthropology a way of seizing the reality of the, to him, strange life lived by the mass of his fellow countryman" (Ibid.:13). The point made by Freedman is valid but good enough to use against his own argument. Taken literally, it implies that most of the studies carried out by sociologists would fall into the category of anthropological studies; after all, sociologists do not always study their own class, or only the elites. And if that were the meaning of distance between the outsider and the "object" society, why have anthropologists in the West not operated nearer home, among their own fellow countrymen constituting the masses? Is it the distinction between the Western and non-Western society that characterizes the discipline of anthropology or the study of the in-group versus the out-group? Obviously, the emergence of Third World anthropologists has created a crisis of definition for anthropology.

The debate regarding the distinction between the two disciplines as it obtains in this region has to be seen in the light of this worldwide trend.

Scholars of this region also seem to be divided on this issue. There are those who maintain the distinction which they have borrowed from the outside, disregarding the realities of their country situation, and there are those who feel that there "is no ground to believe that what appeared reasonable and appropriate under certain conditions will always appear to be so" (Beteille, 1974: 16).

The distinction between these two disciplines is much sharper in the Philippines and in Japan on the one hand, and in Australia and New Zealand on the other. In organizing the chapters of this book for example, a Filipino sociologist, and a Japanese anthropologist, gave identical responses: their inability to cover another discipline. In other countries the situation was not so critical. The Thai scholar prefaces her chapter with these remarks: "The distinction between sociology and social anthropology is seen only by a few. To the majority of people, the distinction is non-existent. In a non-Western society, both sociologists and anthropologists study their own culture and the distinction between sociology and social anthropology disappears" (p. 135). In the Republic of Korea they are treated as "two closely related social science disciplines... Largely sharing the same roots in their prehistory as social science disciplines, sociology and cultural anthropology in Korea have trod their separate paths manifesting quite distinct characteristics in several important aspects, yet maintaining unique overlaps and interrelations between them" (p. 86). Australia maintains the distinction between the two disciplines because of the imposition of the British university structure. In the Philippines, an American cultural anthropologist—John de Young—was appointed by the University of the Philippines to strengthen sociology and he helped separate the two disciplines.

It is interesting that this anthropologist saw a reason for the separate existence of anthropology, but welcomed the idea of himself becoming the chairman of the department of sociology. The Indonesian author informs us: "The assertion common among Indonesian anthropologists and sociologists alike is that there are no differences between the two, except perhaps with respect to the self appellation of their profession and expertise."

Koentjaraningrat has summarized the Indonesian situation very aptly:

> One group was very much in favour of sociology as compared with anthropology. They considered anthropology inappropriate for a growing country, which has to look to the future rather than pay attention to its backward, primitive, and static aspects... Another category, however, recognized the importance of anthropology as a means of acquiring knowledge of and insight into an area with a large diversity of ethnic groups, while they also recognized the advantages of the anthropological method of qualitative inquiry and observation in socio-cultural research in a country with a large proportion of illiterates and peasants among its population...
>
> Concerning their subject matter and field of study, both anthropology and sociology in Indonesia study urban as well as rural problems, although it has been suggested that anthropology in Indonesia should concentrate mainly on socio-cultural problems at a regional level, and sociology on socio-cultural problems at a national level. This division of labour, however, turns out to be hard to maintain. Some Indonesian anthropologists still insist that anthropology is more holistic in its approach, while sociologists tend to look at particular social phenomena and problems. However, if we look at some of the research projects which a number of Indonesian anthropologists are carrying out today, such as cultural aspects of fertility, the economic cost of children in peasant communities, variations in value orientation of students with Chinese school and national school background, comparative study of divorce in peasant and

> urban communities etc.., the above-mentioned distinction become irrelevant.
>
> It might make sense to make some distinction based on the fact that anthropologists indeed have more experience and more adequate concepts to deal with the phenomena of ethnic diversity, but it is my opinion that this is only a matter of training, and it is not difficult to provide students of sociology in Indonesia with concepts and facts which will enable them to cope with similar problems of ethnic diversity in their country...
>
> Despite the large similarity between the two disciplines, the structure of the current Indonesian universities is actually not very conducive to frequent contact between anthropology and sociology. Anthropology departments are part of the Faculty of Letters, whereas sociology departments belong to the Faculty of Social and Political Science. This organization goes back to the Dutch period...
>
> Anthropologists and sociologists are hard to distinguish in Indonesia, except by their difference in educational background. In their profession, they share practically the same knowledge, theories and concepts; are interested in similar national as well as regional problems and in urban as well as rural areas, [and] both utilize similar qualitative as well as quantitative methods (Koenjaraningrat, 1975: 177-78).

The National University of Singapore also does not maintain the distinction. Though the department is designated as that of sociology, it includes anthropology as well. "The character of the department as joint sociology/anthropology department (despite its name!) and the harmonious co-existence of the two disciplines offers particularly favourable conditions for the development of research and training activities", the author of the chapter on Singapore asserts.

In the Indian context, the debate on this issue is largely a part of academic politics related more to the administration and organizational structure of the universities than to the substantive theoretical and methodological issues. The controversy came to the fore when anthropologists began doing village studies. In a previous essay on "The Studies of the Village in India" I dwelt on this, and I quote from it here:

> ....the practitioners of anthropology who were engaged in rural research were the target of considerable criticism by physical anthropologists on the one hand, and sociologists on the other. In the gatherings of the former, they were considered as sociologist-converts because they were no longer studying tribal societies. Some sociologists, in turn, treated them as intruders rather than persons in the same boat. It sounds strange that while the physical anthropologist in his quest for the "missing link" had turned primatologist and had quite justifiably gone down to lemurs and langurs, he hated the legitimate ascendancy of the social anthropologist from the primitives to the peasantry and beyond. As a student of Social Man, the visit of the social anthropologist to a village cannot be regarded as intrusion or encroachment either. Sociologists treating him as an outsider, or a renegade, forget the crucial point that no theory of society can be built without examining the varied manifestations of human social behaviour in different kinds of societal arrangements. It seems paradoxical that while the non-village type sociologists found merit in free borrowing from Indological and even scriptural literature, they advocated refusal of visa to serious sociological work done by a fellow anthropologist (Atal, 1976: 153).

Over the years, however, this debate has become sterile. In his UGC national Lectures in Sociology for 1972-73, Andre Beteille dealt with this problem at length, in one full lecture, and concluded:

> I doubt if in the years to come many serious students of society in India will worry greatly about the distinction between sociology and social anthropology except as a problem in academic administration or academic politics (Beteille, 1974: vii).

He raises the issue quite sharply:

> Contrary to what they say, academics are much preoccupied with labels. But if our discussion is to be fruitful we must look into the reality that lies behind the labels. Are the investigations made by sociologists and social anthropologists basically similar or are they basically different? If they are basically similar, then why divide the investigators into two categories and draw an artificial line between them? If they are basically different, then why not maintain the distinction between them consistently and why are people, particularly in India, continually changing roles, appearing now as sociologists and again as social anthropologists?... (Ibid.: I).

The debate regarding the distinction between the two disciplines has not yet died down but it is guided more by administrative considerations and is thus a part of academic politics. Serious researchers do not seem to be bothered about these labels, and even those who vociferously advocate the maintenance of separate boundaries do not deny themselves the opportunities of attending national and international conferences on the other discipline. Such opportunism makes their case still weaker. In an age where the importance of an interdisciplinary approach is being recognized, it seems vulgar to raise artificial boundaries between sociology and social anthropology.

Research Trends

We may now briefly review the trends of research in the two disciplines. There is clear evidence that research in the Asia-Pacific region has entered a new phase. The key features of the new situation are listed as follows:

1. With the increase in the number of trained sociologists and social anthropologists, the research output has increased considerably as is clear from the number of publications—books and research articles, and even new journals. What is more striking is the fact that unlike in the past, when almost all research was done by outsiders coming from the

West, the new research is being carried out by locals as well and in large numbers. Moreover, the outsiders coming to do research now represent a diversity of disciplinary orientations and nationalities. Previously, it was the prerogative of the anthropologists from the society of the colonizer country to study the peoples of the "colony". In the new phase, the so-called "sociologists" from the West have also moved out of their societies to study societies of Asia and with methodologies other than that of simple participant observation used in anthropological investigations. It also implies that new research is no longer confined to tribal communities.

2. While there has been a decline in the number of anthropologists coming from the earlier colonizing country to a given "colony" of the past, the total number of outside researchers has, in fact, increased. Among them, the American are probably the most numerous.
3. The new context has sharpened the debate regarding the relative advantage of research by insiders versus outsiders. Some countries are assiduously following the path of "localization" which requires replacement of outside faculty by locals. Curbs are also being imposed on expatriate research; researchers from abroad are required to obtain a special visa to conduct research and the governments of the host countries make it obligatory for the researchers to provide them with a copy of their report as also a complete set of data. Such control and monitoring has deterred several scholars from carrying out research in other countries. It has, however, made it possible for outsiders to become attached to national academic institutions and work in collaboration with local scholars.
4. For the Asian scholars greater opportunities now exist for doing work in their own countries. Resource constraints, as also rules regarding expatriate research, do not encourage them, however, to undertake research in other countries of

the region. There is, therefore, very little by way of cross-cultural comparative research undertaken by Asian sociologists and social anthropologists.

5. Priorities of research are being redefined in terms of national needs and social relevance. The availability of funds is also crucial. All this has resulted in the primacy of action-oriented research projects.
6. The influence of American sociology appears to be the strongest in almost all the countries. As a reaction to this, one also observes the growth of Marxism and Marxist sociology.
7. The new sociologists and anthropologists seem to be less concerned with theory building; work is done following borrowed theoretical models, concepts, and methodology. Although the inadequacy and non-suitability of these is debated and discussed in the academic fora, the survey reveals little evidence of the existence of any alternatives. Perhaps the disciplines are going through a reactive and self-searching phase, and have not reached the threshold of alternatives.
8. The creation of professional associations and publication of journals has facilitated communication among colleagues and increased the volume of publications.
9. Research is published not only in the international languages but also in the national languages. This has helped in enlarging the national audience, but at the same time created difficulties in communication with fellow social scientists abroad.
10. With the growth of these disciplines in the region, a greater diversification has resulted in terms of specializations. While earlier research mostly concentrated on descriptive accounts of ethnic communities, the picture today is far more differentiated. In the post Second World War period when these disciplines received recognition in the universities, and when the countries attained independence

and ushered in an era of development, these two disciplines everywhere focussed on rural studies: study of village communities, rural-urban interaction, land reforms and agrarian economy, rural development, and the like. The emphasis on development led to the studies of social and cultural change, and of the process of modernization in general encompassing the trends towards urbanization and industrialization. Subjects that had "practical" or "applied" orientation received priority and the sociologists and social anthropologists became involved in different kinds of action research.

11. In all these countries one finds continuity of interest in the study of traditional structures of kinship, family, and marriage; of folklore, mythology, religion and ritual; of caste and other forms of social stratification.
12. Interest is shown by scholars in the study of inter-ethnic relations, demographic studies (including the study of migration), political sociology, women's studies, study of youth and of old age, industrial and urban sociology, sociology of mass communication, medical sociology, criminology, sociology of education, and sociology of religion. In Indonesia and in Pakistan, a special emphasis is given to the study of Islam. In fact, Pakistan has gone a step forward by introducing Islamic sociology on the one hand and promoting Marxism to encourage class analysis denying the caste paradigm used in the analysis of the neighbouring Hindu society in India.

The above listing is indicative of the diversification that has taken place. The relative importance assigned to these topics varies from country to country. In the countries where the subjects have recently been introduced, research is still largely conducted by foreigners.

In the countries where there is already a long tradition of research, attempts at consolidation and systematization leading to some middle-range theorization are also being made. In such countries, the syllabi include local researches as well. Writing of text books is an important activity for some of the sociologists; for those who are not engaged in research this work is regarded as a "functional equivalent" of research in some countries, while in others text book writing is seen as less prestigious.

Research by Asians has also received international recognition. Many of them have published their books abroad, and have written for the most prestigious professional journals. The Asian-Pacific region has produced sociologists and social anthropologists of international stature; it also has teaching and research centres that have earned worldwide renown.

Problems the Profession Faces

A growing discipline encounters many crises and problems. These relate to the strengthening of infrastructure, establishment of interdisciplinary linkages, and generation and systematization of knowledge. In a way, these problems exist everywhere, in all the countries surveyed in this volume, but their magnitude varies. We will attempt here to identify these problems under the headings suggested above rather than on a country-to-country basis so as to avoid repetition.

Strengthening of Infrastructure

While there are some countries in the region which have still not accorded recognition to sociology and anthropology by granting them status of a university department and instituting postgraduate courses, the countries covered in the volume have more or less resolved this crisis. In each of these countries, there is one or more of these departments—joint departments of sociology and anthropology, or separate for each discipline—although not all universities have them. It is also interesting to observe that wherever anthropology was started first, it included sociology at a later date; but sociology departments have not been equally accommodating. It is also that there are more departments of sociology than of anthropology; consequently the size of the student population graduating in sociology is larger. The identity crisis relative to these disciplines has already been discussed at length in the previous section. Three trends are clearly discernible: (a) a movement away from other disciplines in the social sciences where they were introduced as "papers" or "courses" and the establishment of separate departments; (b) inclusion of their teaching in professional courses in engineering, medicine, and agriculture; and (c) growth of new specialities building new interdisciplinary bridges, e.g., economic sociology, political sociology, medical sociology. All the three developments have created problems for the strengthening of infrastructures to meet the new demands.

(i) Problem of Personnel

In the countries where the disciplines are still young, there is a problem of inadequacy of trained locals; in others, with a relatively longer history, there is the problem of employment and of brain drain. In Indonesia, for example, there are several graduates but only a few professionals. The same is true of Bangladesh, Pakistan, and the Republic of Korea; the problem there is further compounded by the process of so-called "brain drain". It is, however, not so much a problem of locally trained graduates going to other countries; it is rather a problem of the "non-return" of those who had gone abroad for higher studies. Back home they find fewer career openings, less attractive salaries, and discouraging conditions of work. Outside training makes people research oriented, whereas many countries in the region need people to teach courses and share a heavy teaching load, which leaves them with little time to do research. Those who have received training locally are usually deficient in research methodology and in the techniques of electronic data processing, which accounts for the lack of research capability.

Intensive courses in research methodology and in sociological theory are recommended by the authors as a part of the upgrading programme.

(ii) Language Difficulty

Heavy reliance on foreign textbooks has been adversely commented upon by several authors. Because of teaching done increasingly through the medium of the national language, the use of foreign books becomes very restrictive. Even in those countries where English is the medium—Australia, New Zealand—this reliance on external sources is not quite welcome because the foreign text books use illustrative material drawn from quite different settings; the research findings obtained from the country itself do not find a place in them, and thus their relevance is somewhat questioned by the students. This reliance, however, continues because of the dearth of local textbooks. This exists either because competence in the national language to write technical literature is not to be found among the senior scholars who are best qualified to attempt such text books or because the publishing industry in the country does not feel encouraged to print them because of a very limited market.

(iii) Funding Needs

The need for increased financial resources is felt by many. Funds are generally available for applied research and these are given by both government agencies and private foundations—national and foreign. Not many incentives and support mechanisms exist for the individual "odd balls" who wish to do research on esoteric subjects, or concentrate on theoretical work of which the immediate relevance cannot be established. Scholars also question the criteria set for fixing priorities that allow little scope for innovation and bold departures from the set pattern of thinking. Encouragement to such initiatives is deemed by some as a precondition for a healthy growth of the discipline.

(iv) Role of Foreign Researchers

With the change in the composition of the scholarly community, the question of relationship between the outsiders and the insiders comes up quite often. The fact of vertical dependency, and the continuance of superordinate-subordinate relationship is increasingly coming under attack. The presence of foreign researchers without any local institutional attachment is resented, because their research is not immediately made available to the local scholars, and in many cases the young scholars from these countries are recruited by the outsiders only as data collectors rather than full partners in a research undertaking. Government and research organizations now insist, in several countries, that foreigners have an institutional affiliation and that they submit a copy of their research report, as also a set of their raw data.

(v) Lack of Professionalization

Where the disciplines are still young, no professional associations exist to facilitate interaction and communication. Even where they exist they are not always very active. There is a need for seminars, symposia and conferences, and also for the publication of journals. While sociologists and social anthropologists maintain their links with the academic capitals located in the West, which serve as their reference group, very little interaction is to be found within the region. The consequence of this has been academic remoteness among those who are geographically and culturally close.

Japan Sociological Society has made attempts to bridge this distance among Asian sociologists. The "Asian Regional Conference of Sociology" organized in October 1973 by the Japan Sociological Society in collaboration with the Japanese

National Commission for UNESCO "was really the first international meeting of Asian sociologists ever held in Asia". At this meeting, there were participants from the following countries: India, Indonesia, Iran, Republic of Korea, Malaysia, the Philippines, Singapore, Sri Lanka, Thailand, and Japan. The group of Asian sociologists also met at a special session during the World Congress organized by the International Sociological Association in 1978 in Sweden. Again, at the initiative of Japan Sociological Society, another conference of Asian sociologists which focussed on "Comparison of Social Development in Asia" was convened in Japan from October 11 to 13, 1981. The participants came from China, Indonesia, Republic of Korea, the Philippines, Singapore, Thailand and Japan. For anthropologists of the region, the 10th World Congress of Anthropological and Ethnological Sciences held in December 1978 in New Delhi, India, provided the first major opportunity to know and interact with fellow colleagues from within the region.

Problems of an Academic Nature

The authors of these country surveys have also critically reviewed the intellectual contributions made by the practitioners of these two disciplines. They have highlighted the following concerns:

(i) The Need for Indigenization

There is a general feeling that sociology and social anthropology in Asia must not uncritically accept borrowed models, theories and methods, and must attempt to fashion new tools that would be appropriate for the study of these societies. While there are no specific references to any of the borrowed tools, theories, and concepts as regards their non-suitability or appropriateness such criticism of Western sociology seems to be growing. Two attempts to provide alternative models may, however, be noted. In Pakistan, a conscious effort is being made to promote Islamic sociology, and in India some rigorously argue the case for an Indian sociology drawing heavily upon the country's classic tradition that has been studied by the students of Indology. The fact that such suggestions are made, however, should not be taken to mean that all scholars in these countries accept such an alternative formulation, or that there has been a complete boycott of all "external" sociology. As was said before, the disciplines in these countries are going through a reactive phase. As the Korean in the chapter on the Republic of Korea puts it, the need for indigenization is felt as a reaction against their "contamination" by Western methodological orientation (p. 124).

(ii) Lack of Theory

A much repeated fact is that most contributions of the Asians are in the form of descriptive ethnographies or simple statistical analyses. Very little theoretical work is done in the region. Even basic or analytical research into the root causes of the problem has not been attempted. The neglect of history, and "total immersion into the present" is yet other drawback mentioned by the authors.

(iii) Commitment and Social Criticism

Some authors have complained of lack of commitment on the part of sociologists a fact, which is obstructing the path of indigenization and has facilitated uncritical borrowings. To quote from the chapter on the Philippines:

> In recent years the question of whether sociologists should take sides in social issues and advocate their position or not has reportedly cropped up. There are those who continue to take a firm and conscious position of neutrality. To them, the role of the sociologist is mainly to analyze sociology and its dynamics. On the other hand, another group argues that sociologists should

> take the initiative for commitment and active leadership in advocating measures for the betterment of society and espousing the cause of the poor, the downtrodden, and the minorities (pp. 226-27).

Obviously, the issue is unresolved and there does not seem to be any consensus about it. There is vagueness about the question of commitment. Those who advocate the need for social criticism, view commitment in a different light from those who make out a case for committed research. Criticism as a goal implies commitment to criticize anything that belongs to the so-called establishment. Those who take a "constructive" approach talk of commitment to goals and values of the status-quo; even when they do not talk so, it is implicit in their posture. Under attack are those scholars who do research that is commissioned, or just funded; it is argued that all research done for money makes it suspicious and perhaps of low academic quality. The entire question of "academic freedom" is associated with this debate. It can only be said that this is a problematic domain in the area of sociology of knowledge, and deserves serious study.

Conclusion

Sociology and social anthropology in the Asia-Pacific region have come of age. More and more research carried out by locals have, on the one hand, filled several gaps in our knowledge, and, on the other, raised substantive theoretical and methodological issues. The need to organize the vast reservoir of data and knowledge is strongly felt, in the absence of which the hiatus between knowledge produced and knowledge imparted cannot be bridged. The crucial question of the contribution made by these specialities to policy and to planning needs to be examined.

While there is a good deal of discussion about the need for indigenization, there is little evidence of the growth of a new and different style of research. The corrosive effects of academic politics and the pressures to borrow particular lines of research have influenced the development of the two disciplines. The dialogue between the researchers and the policy makers will have to be strengthened and greater interaction between scholars within the region will have to be fostered.

The new issues and new challenges require an interdisciplinary orientation. To achieve this it is not simply a question of sociology and social anthropology giving up their boundary dispute, they should also welcome more interaction with other disciplines engaged in the study of man and society such as economics, psychology, and political science. It is heartening that such an orientation is developing increasingly among the younger generation. Their contributions will hopefully guide sociology and social anthropology to a desirable destination.

Notes

1. It is interesting to note that in India, the leading school of social work in Bombay is also designated as Tata Institute of Social Sciences. This institute offers Master's degree only in social work.
2. Science of Language, and People.
3. Professor M.N. Srinivas told me that Eggan's predecessor in Chicago was Fay Cooper Cole—an archaeologist-ethnologist who did his fieldwork in the Philippines. After about 20 years, Cole gave all his field notes to Eggan. Srinivas' information is based on oral communication from Radcliffe-Brown.

References

Atal, Yogesh (ed.), 1974, *Social Sciences in Asia*, Abhinav Publication, New Delhi.

Atal, Yogesh, 1976, *Social Sciences: The Indian Scene,* Abhinav Publications, New Delhi.

Atal, Yogesh, 1981, "The Call for Indigenization" in *International Social Science Journal,* Vol. XXXIII, No. I, pp. 189-97.

Beteille, Andre, 1974, *Six Essays in Comparative Sociology,* Oxford University Press, Delhi.

Craig, E.W.G., 1964, *Man of the Mist: A Biography of Elsdon Best,* A.H. and A.W. Reed, Wellington.

Freedman, Maurice, 1978, "Social and Cultural Anthropology" in *Main Trends of Research in the Social and Human Sciences*, Part II, Vol. I, pp. 3-176, UNESCO and Mouton, Paris.

Fukutake, T. and Morioka, K., 1974, *Sociology and Social Development in Asia,* University of Tokyo Press.

Koentjaraningrat (ed.), 1975, *The Social Sciences in Indonesia,* Indonesia Institute of Science (LIPI), Jakarta.

Koyano, Shogo, 1974, "Trends in Japanese Sociological Studies" in *Sociology and Social Development in Asia* (ed. Fukutake and Morioka), University of Tokyo.

Pieris, Ralph, 1969, "The Implantation of Sociology in Asia" in *International Social Science Journal,* vol. XXI, No. 3.

Pieris, Ralph, 1976, *Social Development and Planning in Asia,* Abhinav Publications, New Delhi.

3

Sociology in the Indian Campus

A growing discipline passes through various phases. It begins its journey as an illegitimate child; in due course it gets institutionalized; it begins to wear a professional look; and then it starts participating in the culture of romance with other disciplines. The living discipline, thus, remains endogamous only for a little while; its strength lies in its being heterogamous. Sociology had the same story.

Sociology in India, as elsewhere, began its career with the hybrid vigour. The pioneers drawn from fields as distinct as economics, anthropology, indology, and social philosophy worked hard to establish the claim of this discipline through their own research, and through subtle infiltration of sociological orientation in the courses taught by them. Their students constituted the first pressure group for the recognition of sociology as a separate discipline by the Indian universities. Among the old universities, only two were bold to grant this status to sociology—Bombay and Lucknow. These were the centres which supplied the manpower in the initial phase. In the new centers, scholars trained in Bombay and Lucknow carried the tradition of their parent department. Sociology began to grow: more departments, more teachers, more students, more research, and more publicity.

As of now, the sociology enterprise is impressive in size. According to a University Grants Commission (UGC) Report, there were as many as 49 university departments, and 34 departments in affiliated colleges in the country, in the year 1969-70, which imparted postgraduate education in sociology. We may add to this figure, about 15 departments of anthropology. Teaching of sociology in the curricula of institutes of management, and of technology, is in addition to the above enumeration. Postgraduate enrolment in that year alone was 4,918—taking sociology (4,442) and anthropology (476) together—which constituted 11.57 per cent of the total enrolment for postgraduate education in social sciences (42,479). For Ph.D., however, the percentage is a little higher (16.34); of the 2,153 students enrolled for Ph.D. in social sciences, 352 were in the field of sociology alone. The UGC report mentions the figure of 2,582 for the social science faculty of postgraduate departments in universities and colleges; of this number, 243 are sociologists and 119 anthropologists, constituting 14 per cent of the total.

Until 1971, the country had produced a total of 483 doctoral theses in the fields of sociology, social anthropology, criminology and social work; since 1968, the average rate of Ph.Ds. in sociology is 46 per year. This is an impressive figure indeed, compared to the figures for previous periods—thus only four Ph.Ds. were produced during the decade 1931-40, 34 in the subsequent decade; and 79 in the decade 1951-60. There are more than a hundred Ph.Ds. from the universities of Uttar Pradesh and of Maharashtra; other states have the following totals (up to 1970): Bihar (43), Delhi (42), Madhya Pradesh (23), Gujarat (15), West Bengal (14), Rajasthan (12), Punjab (9), Karnataka (7), and others (13).

I have flourished some statistics relative to sociology to highlight the phenomenon of a sudden expansion of the sociology establishment in the country; this is evident, no matter what indicator we choose. The doubling period of sociology is getting smaller and smaller. Before we turn to an examination of the questions that such a situation poses, I will like to relate one more feature of the growth of the discipline. Wherever the discipline was launched, it initially attracted large student clientele—novelty creates a magnetic field for itself. But over a period of time, the student population at each center began to register a decline; in the process, sex composition of the classroom has also changed. In old departments, one finds more female faces—a point that the 1971 census sample has clearly supported. During the annual conference of Kerala Sociological Society, I discovered the same phenomenon. In that state, sociology, perhaps, is going to follow the pattern of matrilineal descent.

The manner in which the profession of sociology is growing has posed a number of pedagogic problems. I would like to describe them as a series of crises, all coexisting, and all requiring immediate attention of the profession. These are: (1) identity crisis, (2) crisis of knowledge generation, and (3) crisis of knowledge dissemination.

Identity Crisis

Sociology has established its identity as a distinct discipline. The word now rings a bell even in lay ears. It has raised high hopes. Of the several problems that plague the country, there are many which are said to have a "sociological dimension". Using this word as a prefix to any issue in question has become quite common. Thus, several kinds of sociologies have begun to rent the air—ranging from a sociology of economic development to a sociology of cow dung. A sociologist today is consulted on a wide range of problems—from abortion to assimilation, from crime to communication, from planning to prostitution, from religion to revolution, and from war to welfare. Looked at this way, sociology has arrived; lay people feel that it has a panacea for all social ills, and they expect it to perform wonders. Today, the problem is not that the discipline has been neglected, it is rather over-recognized—thanks to the salesmanship of the senior cadre, we have oversold our bill of goods. Neither does sociology have in stock answers to the myriad questions on a variety of topics, nor do we have adequate supply of manpower and resources to tackle all of them. The situation is, no doubt, challenging; and there is an opportunity for the discipline to grow. First, a much more differentiated programme of training is necessary to prepare a new generation of sociologists for varied roles, and secondly, researches are required to be undertaken on several themes that are of national importance. A fresh agenda for the development of the discipline is very much in order.

There are many facets of the identity crisis: recognition, credibility, distinctiveness, to mention a few. Recognition crisis is largely resolved. Sociology has been schooled, and is no longer a sporadic activity by a "defector" from another discipline; degrees in sociology are awarded by the universities. Credibility crisis is, however, not completely over. Because of the name semblance, a sociologist is quite often expected to be a socialist or at least a social reformer. On account of heavy reliance on textbooks published in the United States, sociology is treated as "ideology of capitalism" and "supporter of the status quo." Critics of the discipline—both insiders and outsiders—single out the structural-functional approach as the key culprit. In its place, two different brands of historical approach are recommended: Marxian and Indological. Empiricism and survey research have come under heavy fire; a *committed* sociology has also been advocated.

Efforts are also being made by some scholars in the profession to install insulations and make the discipline an impenetrable fortress. In the sixties, the recurrent theme of most symposia and seminars was the distinction between anthropology and sociology. The unending and rather sterile controversy prompted many serious-minded scholars to give it up, while this continues to haunt some of the puritans in the profession.

Sociology in the West is consciously trying to deparochialize itself; there is a quest for a sociology which is globally applicable. Much of the existing theory emanating from the experience of the Western society requires to be tested in other cultural settings. Sociology is thus crossing the boundaries of a single country, as also its own disciplinary boundaries. We have now a spurt in comparative research, and a much more meaningful dialogue with other social science disciplines. In the process, sociology and social anthropology have practically become synonymous and various new branches have developed indicating heterogamy, for example, political sociology, economic sociology, sociology of mass communication, and so on. As against this trend, a section of the Indian scholarship is favoring a deliberate de-universalization of the discipline. Both the attempts, namely, maintaining distance between sociology and anthropology, and advocacy for an Indian sociology are steps in that direction.

Quarrel over boundaries is a political game; surely it is extra-academic. In a country which has to settle several of its pressing problems, altercation among the academics over trivia is nothing but a wasteful and dispensable luxury. If the experience of the past many years is any guide, no single academic discipline can remain aloof, and provide implementable solutions to the problems of various kinds. Problems are not discipline-bound; they are multi-facet, and require a multidisciplinary, interdisciplinary, or even a transdisciplinary approach. Those engaged actively in research and in problem solving have recognized this fact and are least concerned with disciplinary labels. A new breed is growing, which can only be described by the appellation, *social scientist.* This group is trying to integrate the wisdom of the different disciplines and is utilizing methodological apparatus that suits the situation; in the process many bold innovations have been introduced and new theoretical insights have been contributed.

The upcoming generation of social scientists should not be kept in the dark about these developments.

It is also necessary to guard against misplaced chauvinism often expressed in terms of a demand for an independent Indian sociology. This will cause an ethnocentric bias in our approach denying what sociologists have accomplished all over the world. Pleading for a sociology which will have nothing in common with sociology elsewhere is to argue for anti-sociology or a non-sociology. No sociologist disputes the unique character of any given society—not only Indian but any society, for that matter, has its unique configuration as a result of various historical factors and circumstances.

Nevertheless, uniqueness does not imply non-comparability. No two individuals are identical either in their physical appearance or psychological make-up. For that reason, the existence of the sciences of physiology, anatomy, and of psychology cannot, however, be challenged. This is so with sociology which, in essence, is a comparative study of social structures and social processes—processes that tend to maintain social structures, and also change them. Such a focus does not disallow re-examination and verification of the existing body of theory, or refinements, and even addition of concepts, or innovations in the field of methodology. There is consensus among scholars that there are bearings of theory on empirical research. Yet this is different from selling Indology in the name of sociology; or designating Manu and Gandhi as sociologists. Sacred scriptures of the past are no doubt an invaluable source material, but Manu's prescriptions cannot be taken as descriptions of an actually existing social reality of Manu's time, and certainly not of the contemporary era. The controversy raised in the pages of *Contributions to Indian Sociology* by Louis Dumont and David Pocock is interesting and instructive, but the opinion of the profession is more in accord with F.G. Bailey's stand. Indian sociology can be interpreted only to mean sociological analysis of Indian society, it is irrelevant to consider whether the concepts and methodology have originated in India or not, and whether the sociologist is an Indian national or not.

Indian sociology is distinctive only in terms of its focus and research emphasis. The strategy of parochialization is not a proper response to the parochial sociology of the West. There is a case for an overall deparochialization so that the way is paved for a universal sociology.

Crisis of Knowledge Generation

While there exists a "felt need" for sociological expertise, the existing repertory of sociological researches relative to India does not possess answers to the numerous and varied questions. The tradition of research is still recent, and there are many virgin territories to be explored. Western stereotypes about Indian society, dated ethnographic accounts, and prescriptive protocol of sacred writings of ancient sages, cannot all be mixed in one bag and labelled as portrayal of the present day Indian society. A scrutiny of the available researches on Indian society leads one to classify the themes as *more researched, somewhat researched,* and *not-at-all researched.* A long list of researchable topics can be prepared which the available manpower has not been able to exhaust. This is so for a number of reasons; first, many of the sociology-trained individuals lack motivation for research; secondly, research facilities needed for handling several problems, and large-scale surveys are limited; thirdly, excessive load of teaching in colleges and universities leaves very little time for research; and, fourthly, the prevalent bureaucratic ethos of our university system throttles the enthusiasm for research among the younger faculty. It is widely known that in many cases research projects are operated by the heads of the departments who can exercise their manipulative capabilities in getting financial support, while younger scholars are discouraged by several obstacles put in their way.

It is rather unfortunate that the university is increasingly being identified as a conservative force ejecting out research-minded scholars, who are trying to find refuge in newly created research institutes. These institutes provide a better atmosphere for research, and are free from the politics of disciplinary separation and insulation—they provide excellent forum for interdisciplinary dialogue. While this trend is favorable for the growth of knowledge, it must cause worry to the university system and prompt it to initiate steps to stop evaporation of its "think-tank".

Fixing priorities for research is not an easy task. This is an issue on which consensus cannot be reached. It is not only a question of choosing between "disciplinary demands" and "national needs" to define "relevant research"—the two are not necessarily contradictory; differences exist in regard to the problems that deserve a priority treatment. What a funding agency regards as a problem of national significance may be disputed by other scholars. Often enough, one hears scholars mentioning neglected themes, which, according to them, should have been researched and studied a long time back. It is quite possible that had their agenda been followed in the past years, another set of scholars would have launched a tirade and accused the researchers of neglect of the topics which are presently described as "over-researched." Disciplinary values, national self-interest, ideological commitment, and individual scholars' idiosyncrasies are some of the factors that come into play when priorities are being fixed. The question of priorities becomes redundant in a country like India where so little has been done, and so much remains to be done: almost any topic is a good candidate for admission into priority inventory.

Crisis of Knowledge Dissemination

Equally important is the question of dissemination of knowledge thus generated. The recipients of knowledge are a differentiated audience. First, there are those who are likely to join the cadre of professionals; then, there are those who are users—present or potential—of social science. In the first case the task is that of training; in the second, there is the responsibility, and an obligation, of the profession to diffuse and disseminate the generalized culture of the social science—its ethos, its *modus operandi,* its plus points, and the role it can perform.

There is a growing interest in social science, particularly in sociology, among people who occupy different offices—the government men, the industrialists, the technologists, the health experts, the police, the educationists, and even the men of religion. Professional sociologists have the responsibility of educating these people regarding the contribution that sociology can make to their vocation, and the help they can seek from sociologists. Already a clientele has been created and sociology has become a part of the professional kit-bag of doctors, agricultural scientists, and engineers. In the institutions of medicine, agriculture, and engineering, there is now invariably some talk of humanities and social sciences. The social scientist has obtained a visa to enter into these territories. This entry is, however, not without problems.

While the invitation has been extended to a sociologist, or any other kind of a social scientist, by the institutions, he is not particularly welcome in such settings. In most cases, he faces a hostile audience in the classroom, and confronts an indifferent faculty. For the student, the reference group is the professional faculty; for the sociologist, the reference group is the university department. Not being trained to tackle such a situation, sociologists have only attempted to transplant conventional courses of the universities. The students want a justification for such an "imposition," which makes demands on their otherwise busy schedule. Paucity of research related to these fields is a major handicap. No wonder, MacIver could not impress a medical student, and Talcott Parsons horrified a textile technologist. There is need to initiate researches that would provide relevant instructional material; it will also be necessary to cull out from the existing body of sociological knowledge those portions which are vocationally significant to the student who is planning to develop his expertise in some other field. Such sociologists will have to be trained who can take on the role of disseminators in "professional" institutions. A study team set up by the Indian Council of Social Science Research (ICSSR) is investigating the status of social sciences in agricultural engineering, and medical education with a view to evolving a strategy for their proper acceptance in such institutions.

Dialogues will also have to be initiated with policymakers, administrators, and industrialists who are no longer in school. This may take several forms—discussions, workshops, short-term training programmes, syndicates, and the like. Efforts at popularizing sociology among the masses are also needed so that people become familiar with the fruits of research, and sociology may penetrate their thought-ways.

The task of training the future generation of sociologists has become much more difficult. The students enrolling for the courses come from varied backgrounds and with different motivations. There are students in postgraduate classes who have had no background in any of the social sciences; there are students who have a background of some other social science, but not sociology; and finally those who have studied sociology at the B.A. level. The courses taught differ from university to university; so that when students graduating from one university join another university for postgraduation, they take time to readjust to the new emphases.

In terms of social status, students can be classed into two broad groups: those with public school background, and those with the government-run school background. This differentiation is more or less identical with language competence—public school boys have facility in English, others suffer from a lack of it. Motivation of female students is usually different from the rest. Very few girls join the courses with a view to pursuing a career, because in their case it is tied with the career of their prospective husbands. For them, high academic degrees become more of an ornamentation; and, perhaps, the best way to utilize their period of waiting.

The "service-class" students perform three difficult roles simultaneously: they run their families, they attend their offices, and they pursue their education. The motivation to join a specific course may be easy admission and hope of clearing the examinations with relative ease. Their interest is in getting a degree, and not in acquiring skills. For, it is the degree that gives the status; it is the degree that improves the chances of promotion. Since M.A. courses are subject-based, they perforce opt for them.

While the audience is so differentiated, the courses are fashioned solely for purposes of specialization. The consequence of such a policy has been very unfortunate. We have many postgraduates in sociology but very few sociologists. Further, appropriate jobs are scarcely available, which in turn causes underemployment and creates an adverse climate for the subject as also for the new entrants. The problem is also aggravated by the fact that many universities and colleges have failed to attract a good faculty.

Emphasis on teaching through the regional language, and recruitment only of the "sons of the soil," have detracted many scholars from searching for employment in a region other than their own. "Son of the soil" is an ascriptive criterion; its use in the academic context can have disastrous consequences, particularly when the word "soil" is defined in a narrow sense. Insistence on teaching through the regional language also performs the function of keeping away all the so-called "outsiders".

Acceptance of the regional language as the medium of instruction has three implications: it makes extra demands on the teaching community; it necessitates production of literature in the regional languages; and restricts the wider reading ability of the student, thereby creating an intellectual lag as the students are unable to study the recent contributions in other languages. The key question in regard to the language policy relates to the equation between the aims of education and the claims of language. Education aims at, first, imparting information, secondly, disciplining the mind for systematically tackling various problems, and, thirdly, inculcating the spirit of discovery. For these aims, language is only a means. Since sociology developed mainly in the West, most of the books are available in non-Indian languages. Sociology reaches the Indian student through the gateway of English. Most of the students now entering postgraduate departments have received education through their vernacular languages. This sudden switchover to English puts them in a disadvantageous position.

Among the teachers, too, we have three different sets: (1) those who had all their education through English language; (2) those who had most of their education through English but who are proficient in their regional language; and (3) those who have graduated in sociology through an Indian language.

With slight adjustments, this classification may also stand for the generation differences. In a country where seniority goes largely with age, one may expect that all senior positions in the departments of sociology are occupied by people belonging to category one. Barring those who can competently communicate through the regional language also, most of the senior professors feel diffident to use any language other than English in their professional work. The other extreme (category three) consists of people who find it difficult to comprehend fully, material available in English language. They read the material available in the Indian languages, which is, very often, sub-standard. The demand for books in the vernacular could not be fulfilled by seniors who were experts in the field, because they lacked communication skills in vernacular languages. This gave rise to a class of saviours.

In terms of their authorship, the books produced in vernacular languages in sociology can be classified into five categories: (1) Books in which content-level is tolerable, but the language is poor; (2) books in which content-level is poor, and language is journalistic; (3) books which have a fair balance of the two; (4) books which are poor in content as well as language; and (5) books which are competently done—most of these being translations of standard works in English.

It must be said that many of the so-called "original" text books are best examples of plagiarism. The craft of writing a textbook has certain distinguishing features: the subject-matter of these books is determined by the university syllabi; considerable distortion is introduced during the process of transliteration; the emphasis is more on definitions and quotations, and less on explanation; and most often, one particular book originally written in English is used as the base and a vernacular version is prepared in which footnotes are made a part of the text. Produced cheaply, and in large quantities, these books keep the good ones out of circulation. Question-answer type essays, "keys" and "An Hour Before the Examination" series flood the market and the vulnerable student falls an easy prey to these allurements. The beneficiaries are mainly the publishers; the sufferer is sociology. The damage done this way is beyond repair; after a habit of short-cut journey, a long and circuitous route of hard work cannot attract traffic. The existing system of examination with its emphasis on memorizing has fostered this tendency. Induction into sociology through such a backdoor has had a telling effect on the teaching standards. It is the riff-raff sociology that is taught and learned in our colleges. Those centers which have stuck to English have, in the process, become elites; a class-structure has thus emerged in the profession.

Blaming the language policy of the State does not seem to me the answer to the prevailing crisis. What needs to be emphasized is the fact that practitioners of the discipline that focuses on the processes of social change have simply failed to anticipate the situation. They did not make any effort to "manage" this change. Though knowing fully well that in the 1970s the non-English speaking students will knock the doors of the departments, the leaders of the profession remained under the spell of slumber and hoped that their political acumen would avert the crisis. This did not happen; sociology was not applied even in the case of sociology. We have now the students, but we do not have proper teaching material, nor do we have competent teachers in adequate numbers to teach in regional languages. Both these problems need to be tacked immediately.

Today's students are teachers and researchers of the future. For accepting either of the two roles in a region other than one's own, it will be necessary to develop proficiency in some other regional language. The discipline of sociology is such that training in language can be built into the syllabus. This has also been neglected. Rather than insisting on proficiency in German or French before allowing a Ph.D. candidate to submit his thesis, regional languages could have been introduced. Emphasis on cross-cultural research would have automatically forced a student to visit other cultural regions for fieldwork, and thereby learn the language. However, students with modest means will have to be assisted by some kind of financial assistance so as to do their research effectively. This insistence would have served two purposes: first, the student would have been better trained as a researcher with comparative orientation; and, secondly, he would have thus qualified for a job in more regions than one. It is time that we give serious thought to this strategy. Since it does not require any change in the existing statutes of the university, therefore, this task should be undertaken without any further delay.

In a similar fashion, it is possible to make some innovations in the syllabi without affecting the university norms. A teacher may find it difficult to change the entire syllabus, or to introduce new topics in a paper, but he can certainly modernize the content of a topic that is already included in the syllabus; fresh research material and recent publications can be utilized by him. But this is rarely so. An inspection of the syllabi will reveal that publications authored by Indian sociologists are generally ostracized. We still have a fascination for "foreign". What is more striking is the fact that those favouring "Indianization" of sociology have also promoted this policy of exclusion. Wherever the Board of Studies made the bold attempt of introducing new topics, paradoxically, the resistance came from the college teachers on the apparently reasonable plea that there is non-availability of books in their libraries. What remains unstated, however, is the fact that most of them are unwilling to accept the new challenge and update their knowledge. This is rather sad; ignorance is never bliss in the field of knowledge.

Increasing specialization and growing sophistication of research methodology in the field of sociology have made it imperative to develop mechanisms by which scholars continually reorientate themselves, and assimilate new thinking. To introduce advanced methodology in the postgraduate curricula, the first need is to train the faculty. In the past few years, academic style has undergone considerable change. There is more and more use of the language of numbers, and of algebra. The advent of machine culture in research has, on the one hand, enlarged the scope of enquiry and made possible multivariate analysis; and, on the other, made many of our old skills primitive. It is true that there is no need to be servile to the machine, but rejection of a technique without knowing it is a non-rational action.

We did not notice the wave of change a decade ago when local languages started replacing the "international" language. If we still fail to notice what is happening in our schools today, we will be preparing a generation of teachers who will find it difficult to handle the classes tomorrow. What is taught by way of statistics in the postgraduate classes today is also now a part of elementary mathematics at the higher secondary schools. Not only this, the language of set theory so useful in analysis of social phenomena, is now being taught right from the primary school stage. Talking of groups and subgroups, castes and subcastes, role-sets and status-sets becomes much more intelligible if Venn diagrams are used; these are known even to an eighth-standard student. Our future teachers will be in a position to communicate better if this could be learned through some capsule courses.

It is time we give serious thought to the courses taught at the universities. They appear to be discrete, and lack theoretical coherence. Integration of theory, concept methodology, and illustrative content does not exist in our syllabi. Even the available research material from the Indian setting has not been properly integrated in the theoretical framework of sociology. Researches on India are included to teach about Indian society, and not sociology. Indian sociologists are offered faculty positions abroad mainly to teach about India, and only peripherally to teach solid sociology. This is not a particularly happy situation and deserves to be remedied.

Western sociology has started talking of coming crises, can Indian sociology lag behind?

4

Sociology-Anthropology Interface*

I regard this as a distinctive honour to have been asked to deliver this inaugural lecture to mark the introduction of anthropology at this university. For this, I am grateful to your Vice Chancellor, Dr Hari Mohan Mathur. Both of us have been friends since our college days at Udaipur; both of us have graduated in anthropology—he from Lucknow, me from Saugar; and both of us are renegades—he left the academia to join the Indian Administrative Service, and I lost my identity as an anthropologist in my efforts to build bridges between different social science disciplines and in campaigning for demolition of barriers that separate one discipline from another. I can't say about myself but we certainly felt that Dr Mathur's decision to join the civil service was a loss to the academe. But that prophecy was self-cancelled. He continues to be a voracious reader, and his pen still flows to do books of merit. I envy the manner in which he combines the two roles.

Dr Mathur must be congratulated for succeeding in creating a place for anthropology in this university—a dream that he dreamt for quite sometime. Had there been anthropology at the postgraduate level when we did our graduation, perhaps we would not have migrated.

---

* Inaugural address to mark the introduction of Master's Course in Anthropology at the University of Rajasthan, delivered on 15 December, 1988.

It should be said here for record that Rajasthan University pioneered the teaching of anthropology at the undergraduate level, as part of the sociology option. I reminisce with pleasure, and bow down with gratitude to Professor Brij Raj Chauhan who inaugurated the teaching of sociology in Rajasthan at the Maharana Bhopal College, Udaipur. With an M.A. in economics from Lucknow, being a student of academic giants like Professors Radha Kamal Mukerjee, D.P. Mukerji, and D.N. Majumdar, Professor Chauhan single-handedly promoted the cause of sociology, and made anthropology an integral part of the intellectual kit of a sociologist. He made us visit the villages to develop skills in participant observation, and conduct surveys. We were made to read textbooks in geology and zoology to learn about earth's stratification system and the origin and evolution of man. It exalted our ego when we consulted Grey's anatomy textbook that continues to be a must for a medical student. At the B.A. level we familiarized ourselves with Professor M.N. Srinivas' study on the *Religion and Society among the Coorgs of South India*. We had an expose on Professor S.C. Dube's recently published book on the Shamirpet village of Andhra Pradesh. We could talk of *Sanskritization*, of Redfield's *Little Communities*, and of Marriott's work on the processes of *parochialization* and *universalization*. Luckily for us, there were no substandard textbooks in the vernacular, and no half-baked "keys" and "question-answer" books. In our mental frame sociology and social anthropology coexisted as cognate disciplines with inseparable links.

I deliberately chose to begin with such a personal note to underline the recency of anthropology on the academic scene in India. No doubt, investigations on Indian society started much earlier, somewhere in the 18th century by Indologists; but it is only in the latter half of the 19th century that ethnographic compilations of Indian customs and traditions, and descriptive accounts of castes and tribes were undertaken by British administrators and Christian missionaries. While these accounts provided useful information to acquaint the alien administrators, they only represent rudiments of anthropology. They were not academic exercises in the strict sense of the term. The latter day administrators, dissatisfied with rather sketchy accounts of earlier scribes, and inspired by the ethnographies produced by British anthropologists of primitive societies elsewhere, began undertaking detailed studies of the tribes in the areas of their posting. These were joined by overseas researchers, and a few Indians who returned after their training abroad. But still the corpus of knowledge about Indian society was meagre. For example, David G. Mandelbaum said that he began his field research in 1936 with very little to read by way of orientation. For him, "the available resources for such preparation were slim. No American social-cultural anthropologist had then worked in India... A few American missionaries had written ethnographic accounts of particular groups, but the bulk of the ethnological literature had been done by British civil servants, primarily to aid in the colonial administration. There were the 'Castes and Tribes' volumes by Risley, Thurston, Russell and Hira Lal, and others. The district gazetteers and the census volumes, especially the 1931 Census for which J.H. Hutton was Census Commissioner, included a good deal of disparate ethnographic information" (Mandelbaum, 1978: 2). Mandelbaum refers to the work of W.H.R. Rivers on *The Todas* which, for "lack of a better resource... was for decades the one work on an Indian group that was widely used in the teaching of cultural anthropology" in the United States.

Mandelbaum also refers to the work of Henry Maine, A.M. Hocart, T.C. Hodson, C. Bougle and L.S.S. O'Malley which "surveyed broad aspects of Indian society and civilization". But these did not distinguish between "scriptural social prescriptions" and the actually existing social reality. He did not regret not reading then the writings of Max Weber and Karl Marx on India, as these would not have helped him prepare, he admits, for the fieldwork.

This was the situation of anthropological field research in 1937 when anthropologists—both foreign and Indian—were just at the beginning of their fieldwork; from then on, field research gained momentum and several studies were carried out in tribal groups and village communities.

The university system was, however, slow to accord recognition to this discipline. The first department of anthropology was created at Calcutta University in 1917, but the professorship there was instituted in 1920. It took 30 years to establish the second professorship at Lucknow University where its first incumbent—D.N. Majumdar—was appointed as lecturer in primitive economics in 1928 in the department of economics and sociology. Even in 1960, there were only 11 university departments of anthropology with seven full professorships. The number of these departments may have grown over these years but certainly the rate at which sociology has gained recognition is much higher compared to anthropology. Since several sociology departments include teaching of anthropology in their curricula one could combine these figures to assess the real spread of anthropology. In fact, one of the departments of sociology in a leading central university can more appropriately be described as a department of social anthropology, notwithstanding the fact that the same university has a separate and well-established department of anthropology that offers specialization in both physical and social anthropology, as well as in prehistoric archaeology.

Higher education in India followed the British pattern. Being a major colonial empire, scholarship in Britain paid special attention to the study of the cultures of their colonies as they were different, non-Western, queer and exotic, mostly primitive; moreover, they needed their understanding to better administer them. Such studies constituted the domain of anthropology which came to be defined as the study of "other cultures" rather than fulfilling its claim to be a "Mirror for Man" or a speciality devoted to "Man and His Works" at all levels of cultural development. Understandably, British universities were late in according recognition to sociology; social anthropology practised there was regarded as sociology of the primitive peoples. It is worthy of note that Oxford does not still have a department of sociology, and the Cambridge chair in sociology was created only in 1968. One finds a similar pattern in India; the old and established universities have been late in introducing sociology compared to the newly established universities. Since sociology arrived in India mainly via the United States, its practitioners copied the US pattern and consciously distanced themselves from anthropology, so much so that they would not consider a graduate in social anthropology eligible for a faculty position. This holds true of Rajasthan, when Rajasthan University started the department of sociology, it did not invite anthropology applicants even for an interview. I am told that in one of the state-level conferences in, sociology, held in Jaipur a few years ago, a resolution was passed to maintain a safe distance from anthropology. Let me however, hasten to mention that Jodhpur University is an exception. Its first head of the department was a Ph.D. in anthropology, and it still has a faculty member with a degree in that subject. I was myself offered professorship in sociology at that university in 1972. Now with the creation of a chair in anthropology at the Rajasthan University let me hope that further compartmentalization will not occur and that barriers will not be erected between the two disciplines. Should that happen, it will be unfortunate particularly in the present context when the world over interdisciplinarity in social sciences is being emphasized. And I regard anthropology as a truly interdisciplinary discipline having its links both with the social and biological sciences.

It is true that anthropology began as a unifying science of Man. But its claims notwithstanding the discipline of social and cultural anthropology somehow focussed on the primitive and the past, and allowed sociology to concentrate on the Western and the modern. While this division of labour in the Western intellectual tradition may have some merit, it is irrelevant in the intellectual context of the countries of the Third World.

Writing in 1962, S.C. Dube questioned the continuance of the classical grand design of the discipline. He said:

> I am not against a unified and integrated science of Man, nor do I claim that any one part of anthropology is more important than others... I do wish to suggest, however, that the 'grand design' is being sustained more by nostalgia than by logic; accidental factors in the historical growth of the subject appear to have involved us emotionally to such a degree that at present we are unable to foresee clearly the natural and inevitable requirements for the growth of the individual constituents of anthropological studies... The so-called composite courses in the subject claim to lay equal or nearly equal emphasis on the different branches... There are two major objections to such an arrangement. First, the teaching of these independent branches is not sufficiently and imaginatively integrated; the student is often left wondering about their logical connection. Secondly, the burden of the different branches put together is so much that it severely limits the possibilities of specialization available to the student [Dube, 1962: 242].

Maurice Freedman of Oxford also advocates modesty in regard to anthropology's claims. He argues:

> If anthropology were the study of Society and societies, and of Culture and cultures, without qualification, it would be grotesquely encyclopedic, and no men could be found to practice it. Even to suggest that it might tend towards realizing so englobing a plan would be to raise the flag of an intolerable scholastic imperialism... Social and cultural anthropology is for the vast majority of its adherents a practicable subject because it is

> limited in scope—although few, if any scholars can practice all of it... In recent times it has been common enough for anthropologists to class themselves as specialists in (some would say, sociologists of) primitive society, that form of society being in turn defined as non-literate, small in scale, and based upon a simple technology... [Freedman, 1978: 8-9].

In present day anthropology one witnesses a simultaneous operation of two processes: one, effort to delimit the scope of the discipline; and two, increasing specialization of its various branches. Thus, social anthropologists have logically extended their field of enquiry from the study of small, homogeneous, microcosmic folk societies to cover other broader units of social organization. Even while adhering to the study of the tribal societies, which were their traditional domain, they realized that not all tribal societies corresponded to the ideal-type. There are larger, heterogeneous tribal groups as well which have centralized forms of government and complicated technologies. A move from the study of tribes to the study of village communities in complex cultures such as India was a logical one. Such studies required a different conceptual apparatus and several methodological innovations. The village in India became a meeting ground for anthropologists and sociologists—one arriving from the tribe and the other from the city. While their approach remained similar, almost identical, the two insisted on different labels.

The social anthropologist working in the village became a target of attack both by the physical anthropologists and the sociologists. The former regarded him as a defector to sociology, while the latter received him as an intruder. Having reneged myself, I too felt that dual oppression, and expressed my opposition in the following manner:

> It sounds strange that while the physical anthropologist in his quest for the 'missing link' had turned a primatologist and had quite justifiably gone *down* to lemurs and langurs, he hated the legitimate *ascendancy* of the social anthropologist from the

> primitives to peasantry and beyond. As a student of social Man, the visit of the social anthropologist to a village cannot be regarded as an intrusion or encroachment either. Sociologists treating him as an outsider, or a renegade, forget the crucial point that no theory of society can be built without examining the varied manifestations of human social behaviour in different kinds of societal arrangements. It seems paradoxical that while the non-village type sociologists found merit in free borrowing from Indological and even scriptural literature, they advocate refusal of visa to serious sociological work done by a fellow anthropologist [Atal, 1976: 153].

Apart from the subject matter, a distinction is also drawn between sociology and anthropology in terms of the methodology employed. It is generally argued that problems involved in the study of 'other cultures' are different from those entailed in the study of one's own society. There is no dispute about this assertion. But one would like to highlight the fact that this principle of studying 'other cultures' was greatly violated by the leading centres of anthropology located in the West where many of the anthropologists from the Third World countries, including India, received their training. These scholars were sent to their own societies to conduct the field work. These societies are surely 'other cultures' for the Western gurus but not for those who studied them. The Asian students were not encouraged to study the West which would have been the 'other culture' for them. Similarly, it is ridiculous to draw a distinction based on the nationality of the investigator rather than the subject matter of study. The work on caste by J.H. Hutton and by G.S. Ghurye is based on secondary data and library research, yet one is regarded as anthropological and the other sociological. This is, in my view, absurd.

Freedman tries to provide an answer to the criticism about studying one's own society that I have mentioned. He feels that the "distancing between the observer and the observed in the "classical" mode of field study is upto a point reproduced in the relationship between the "new" anthropologist and the people he studies, even though he and they are members of one society. Africa, India, and some countries in Latin America provide very good examples because of their ethnic heterogeneity. Moreover, social scientists are not peasants or workers and are rarely drawn from their ranks. Indeed, it is probably the case that the bourgeois or member of the elite often sees in anthropology a way of seizing the reality of the, to him, strange life lived by the mass of his fellow countrymen" (Freedman, 1978: 13). The point made by Freedman is valid but good enough to use against his own argument. Taken literally, it implies that most of the studies carried out by sociologists would fall into the category of anthropological studies. And if that were the meaning of distance between the outsider and the "object" society why have anthropologists in the West not operated nearer home, among their own fellow countrymen constituting the masses?

Let me also quote the remark on the distinction between sociology and social anthropology made by Andre Beteille in one of his UGC lectures in 1972-73. Regarding this debate purely as a problem in academic politics, Beteille said:

> Contrary to what they say, academics are much preoccupied with labels. But if our discussion is to be fruitful we must look into the reality that lies behind the labels. Are the investigations made by sociologists and social anthropologists basically similar or basically different? If they are basically similar, then why divide the investigators into two categories and draw an artificial line between them? If they are basically different, then why not maintain the distinction between them consistently and why are people, particularly in India, continually changing roles, appearing now as sociologists and again as social anthropologists?... [Beteille 1974: 1].

All this must suffice to settle the meaningless dispute. But I feel tempted to allude to some more statements to further cement my observation.

Don Martindale, a famous American sociologist, wrote in 1961:

> ... Apart from differences which emerge directly out of its peculiar historical context, it would be hard to say in what manner in the long run the theories of anthropology will differ from those of sociology [Martindale, 1961: 44].

Reflecting on the relationship between the two disciplines in the context of India, T.B. Bottomore has this to say:

> ... as the primitive societies regarded as the preserve of the social anthropologist have more or less disappeared so to some extent the special prerogatives of the sociologist in studying advanced societies have been challenged. Among contemporary societies, there is a very important category of those which are neither primitive nor industrially advanced. In such societies, of which India is an outstanding example, the distinction between sociology and social anthropology has little meaning... There is a real opportunity in India for the traditional division between these disciplines to be overcome... The development of social sciences in India and the diminishing dependence upon foreign educational resources will give an opportunity for a real integration of the methods and concepts of two disciplines in terms of the problems and research tasks relevant to Indian social life [Bottomore, 1962: 58].

The Review Committee on Sociology, appointed by the University Grants Commission in 1961, also reiterated the same point by recommending:

> That in universities which already have strong departments of sociology, social anthropology should be developed within their fold. On the other hand, in universities with sociologically-oriented departments of social anthropology, it would be an advantage to initiate studies in sociology within their fold.

The decision to create a chair in anthropology within the department of sociology at this university is thus a welcome initiative. It would provide an effective ground for active interchange between the practitioners of twin disciplines. The graduates of this department will have the opportunity to acquaint themselves with the contributions to theory and to the understanding of Indian society made by the previous generations of sociologists and social anthropologists. They will find merit in going beyond the conventionally defined territories of the two disciplines. The advantage of interdisciplinary orientation will be felt by them.

It needs to be reiterated that anthropology as a discipline is a *federal* science. It should not be viewed as a mere assemblage of different disciplines and a patch work of elements drawn from various branches of knowledge. It is not a little bit of everything. It is not unique because of its encyclopaedic coverage. It is not a junction point of disciplines engaged separately in the investigation of the various facets of Man. A conceptual integration at a higher level to view human life in its totality, emphasizing a holistic perspective, characterizes the anthropological outlook. An anthropologist is, at times, described as a man having several "skills in one skull". The guiding principle of the discipline is *comparison*: man as a biological being compared to other animals; present-day Man compared to his predecessors in an evolutionary sequence; people of one race compared to others; comparison of cultures in time and space. Although having such a comparative perspective, the various constituents of this science have moved towards a greater degree of specialization and autonomy. General anthropologists of the previous years are now a vanishing tribe. A specialist in one of the branches of anthropology receives basic orientation in other branches so as not to lose the integrative principle and the focus on comparison, but his specialization creates conditions for closer interaction with those disciplines that are also engaged in the exploration of that territory. Thus physical anthropologists share much in common with practitioners of biological sciences; ethnologists are coming closer to historical sciences; and social anthropologists are dialoguing with sociology and other social sciences. In fact, social anthropologists are becoming a synonym for comparative sociologists. The distinction drawn between the study of one's own culture and society (sociology) and of 'other' cultures and societies (anthropology) has relevance only in this regard. An exposure to other cultures improves one's understanding of one's own society and culture. Anthropology helps in curbing ethnocentrism and in developing cultural relativism.

The present-day social anthropology has evolved through several phases. It began as a history of Man and his culture and concentrated on the reconstruction of evolutionary stages. Dealing with preliterate and primitive societies much of this work was conjectural. In its second phase, social anthropology redefined itself as geography of man and culture, trying to map the distribution of material cultural traits, spread of people along racial lines, and drawing of cultural areas. From there, it moved, in the third phase, towards comparative sociology which resulted in the development of conceptual frameworks and theoretical sophistication. Lately, psychological and philosophical orientations were added to anthropological research. With the end of the colonial era and introduction of planned social and cultural change by the newly independent states, diagnostic and therapeutic orientation was added to anthropology, giving rise to applied and action anthropology. Social anthropology got involved in the investigation and theorizing of social change.

Indian anthropology has responded to these changing orientations. Fads and fashions in the profession have guided their research priorities. While it is important to follow the trends and be conversant with them it is equally necessary to occasionally attempt a stock-taking exercise. There is a need to critically estimate the researches done, carefully plan future research work, and comparatively evaluate the syllabi and courses of study. There was a time when no one would have qualified as a social anthropologist without doing field research in a tribal community. Today it is rather sad that research on tribes and on village communities is going out of fashion. One also does not notice any significant trend towards the study of societies other than India. There is enough scope for revisiting the Indian tribes and villages not only to prepare conventional ethnographic monographs but to attempt different kinds of studies using new conceptual apparatus and modern methodology. The task of studying tribes should not be left solely with the institutes of tribal research or the Anthropological Survey of India; the universities must continue to provide the lead.

For this, teaching must also be imaginatively planned. Introduction of anthropology as a subject of teaching at M.A. level would require suitable adjustment in the university curricula. In our anxiety to enlarge and modernize the curricula so as to provide an interdisciplinary orientation, there is a danger to make the courses cumbersome, logically disconnected, and impractical. It would be necessary to imaginatively devise courses and work out their contents rather than follow the stereotype courses. At the same time, the teaching of anthropology need not be confined to sociology alone; as part of liberal education, courses in anthropology may be offered in other social science disciplines as well.

The task of doing this is challenging and worthwhile. Let me hope that the arrival of anthropology will not accentuate academic wrangle, and that social sciences at this university will flourish in an atmosphere of amity.

References

Atal, Yogesh, 1976, *Social Sciences: The Indian Scene*, Abhinav Publications, New Delhi.

Atal, Yogesh (ed.), 1985, *Sociology and Social Anthropology in Asia and the Pacific*, Wiley Eastern, ; New Delhi. and UNESCO Paris.

Beteille, Andre, 1974, *Six Essays in Comparative Sociology;* Oxford University Press, Delhi.

Bottomore, T.B., 1962, *Sociology: A Guide to Problems and Literature*, Allen and Unwin, London.

Dube, S.C., 1962, "Social Anthropology: India" in *Indian Anthropology: Essays in Memory of D.N. Majumdar* (edited by T.N. Madan and Gopala Sarana), Asia Publishing House, Bombay.

Freedman, Maurice, 1978, "Social and Cultural Anthropology" in *Main Trends of Research in the Social and Human Sciences* Part II, Vol.1, UNESCO, and Mouton, The Hague.

Mandelbaum, David G., 1978, "New Directions for South Asian Anthropology" in *American Studies in the Anthropology of India* (edited by Sylvia Vatuk), Manohar Publications, New Delhi.

Martindale, Don, 1961, *Nature and Types of Sociological Theory*, Routledge and Kegan Paul, London.

5

The Call for Indigenization*

Social science growth in the Third World is to be seen in the context of the twin processes of decolonization and development that are simultaneously in operation. Born together in the same historical moment, capitalism, colonialism, and social sciences arrived from the West and became implanted in those countries that became colonies of the Western powers. Academic colonialism, in fact, went beyond the boundaries of political colonies; countries that managed to retain their political autonomy could not prevent the vicarious colonization of their academia. The westernization/ modernization package had a much wider clientele. The relationship of "dependency, deference and servility" created and maintained through these processes is now under attack. Planners and policy makers of the developing world are finding faults with the Western paradigm of development, and social scientists are articulating their dissatisfaction with Western theories and methodologies. There is a certain revolution of relevance. Development strategists are sloganizing the need for endogenous development; social scientists are agonizing about indigenization.

---

* Reproduced from *International Social Science Journal*, Vol.XXXIII, No.1, 1981, pp.189-197.

The question of indigenization has been discussed in several national and international meetings organized under different auspices. The movement began to gain momentum in the early 1970s when indigenous scholars from the Third World raised their voice against the implantation of social sciences perpetuating "captivity" of mind; they were joined by a number of social scientists from Western countries sharing this concern. In Asia, the concern was most eloquently expressed at the first Asian Conference on Teaching and Research in Social Sciences, organized under UNESCO auspices in 1973 at Simla, India. Again, in a meeting on Interregional Cooperation in the Field of Social Sciences, organized by UNESCO in Paris in 1976, the participants underlined the fact that 90 per cent of the social scientists of the world came from the developed countries. To quote from the report of the meeting (UNESCO, 1977: 8):

> It is not merely the fact of a linkage that is noteworthy, but more so the fact that in the case of the developing regions, it is a relationship of dependency: to put it in other words (repeatedly used at the meeting), it is a 'vertical' relationship between the donors and recipients, between patrons and clients. . . . Though practically all the Third World Countries are now politically independent, 'self rule' in the field of social sciences remains still to be achieved. . . . [The] numbers of indigenous social scientists have undoubtedly increased but they are more in contact with their Western colleagues than with their counterparts in the Third World or, for that matter, even within their own region; the questions these social scientists ask, the paradigms and research techniques they employ, the vision they have of the future of their countries—all these are for the most part imported from the West, or at best adapted from the work of Western thinkers including social scientists. No wonder, then, that social sciences in the Third World are often judged to be irrelevant and the social scientists accused of being alienated from their societies.

The question of indigenization was also taken up by the Conference of National Social Science Councils and analogous bodies (CNSSC), at its 1977 meeting. In 1978, the Wenner-Gren Foundation organized a conference on indigenous anthropology. The Korean Social Science Research Council convened a seminar to discuss "Koreanization of Western Approaches to Social Sciences" in early 1979. In September 1979, the Association of Asian Social Science Research Councils (AASSREC) organized in collaboration with CNSSC—now renamed International Federation of Social Science Organizations (IFSSO)—a special panel discussion during its Third Conference held in Manila.

There is, thus, a worldwide concern with this problem. This article attempts to synthesize the major trends of thinking and articulates key concerns related to the call for indigenization.

The call for indigenization of social sciences in Asia has not yet gone beyond the reactive phase. Since these reactions come from different sources, albeit all from the professional social scientists, they emphasize different aspects of indigenization. Even the definitional crisis has not yet been resolved: indigenization means different things to different people.

The social sciences in Asia and the Pacific are at different stages of development. Their introduction to individual countries was determined by their respective colonial masters. The period of their entry, the relative emphasis given to different disciplines, the "external" orientation of the first generation of native social scientists, and the literature on the society and culture of these countries are all influenced by the colonial heritage. Even those countries that were not colonized politically have gone through a process of what may be called vicarious colonization through which external influences permeated their societies and cultures.

Under the colonial regime, a single-aperture model was in operation: influences from outside came largely through a single gateway, namely the metropolitan country. The post-colonial phase saw an attempt to establish a multi-aperture model: while not fully closing the previous aperture, a conscious effort was made to be receptive to several sources of inspiration and influence. An effort to break the links with the former colonizer and yet not to become completely insulated from the outside was then attempted.

An essential ingredient of the process of decolonization is the emphasis on endogeniety and on acceleration of the pace of development in the direction supposedly determined by the national government. In some countries, this process of decolonization started long before the attainment of independence, in others it began much later, even after independence. This difference notwithstanding, all of them have a certain degree of ambivalence towards their former rulers. Such love-hate relationship is noticed even in the case of the social sciences.

While the need for the upgrading of social scientists and the improvement of the quality of social science is recognized, the former colonies have attempted to locate overseas academic capitals, mainly in the English-speaking world. Such a transition was easier for those countries who had English-speaking rulers; for others, this posed problems particularly of communication. The initiation of the development era attracted foreign experts, both as part of "aid" packages and as scholars interested in the study of directed change in societies other than their own. This put an end to the monopoly enjoyed by the social anthropologists who were previously alone among social scientists in specializing in the study of "other cultures".

At the political level, the decolonization process was spelt out as the process of localization or nativization. It is this sense in which Jawaharlal Nehru, and his compatriots, for example, raised the slogan for Indianization during the freedom struggle. At present, such demands are most vociferously made by the small island nations of the Pacific. Although they have attained independence, their services are mostly manned by outsiders, generally coming from a single country. As a part of their localization drive, they have started putting severe restrictions on expatriate research; they do not wish to remain subjects of study, like museum specimens. Rather than being portrayed by an outsider, they would prefer their own scholars to provide an insider's view of reality; instead of encouraging research on esoteric aspects of their culture by outsiders, they would prefer systematic investigation of relevant problems that are assigned priority by themselves. The evaluation of proposals for research submitted by expatriates is now being made by many Asian countries and is regarded by them as a necessary step towards promotion of "relevant research". Thus, at the political level, indigenization stands for localization, control and monitoring of expatriate research, and promotion of research on relevant themes.

Academics have also joined the chorus in favour of indigenization. In its extreme formulation, the demand appears almost like a revolt against the dominance of Western concepts, theories and methodologies, which are decried as "unsuitable" and "irrelevant" in the Asian context. They criticize, on the one hand, the quality of work done by foreigners on their societies, and, on the other, the blind imitation of foreign models by local scholars who have been trained abroad. It is argued that there is considerable distortion of facts and misrepresentation of reality in the writings of outsiders; seeing it with a different cultural lens, they are unable to go beyond the surface and detect deeper meanings. Worse still, political and ideological motivations are imputed to foreign scholars who are seen as promoters of a homogenizing, convergence model, as practitioners of some kind of "Project Camelot", as maintenance engineers of a superordinate/subordinate relationship. Western social science is viewed by some as a kind of octopus.

Severe criticism of "borrowed consciousness" is to be found in the writings of those social scientists who have attempted forcefully to articulate the demand for indigenization.

In a 1968 symposium on "The Relevance of Social Sciences in Contemporary Asia" (organized by the World Student Christian Federation), several speakers dwelt on this theme. For example, Kikuo Yamaoka (Japan) (1968:4) remarked:

> We Asian scholars have done little more than import the several social sciences directly from the West, and use them to prepare and deliver our lectures, but have failed to give birth to creative theories designed for, and derived from, Asian realities.

In a much stronger language, C. T. Kurien (India) (1968: 17-18) declared:

> We are neither Asian nor scientists. Our knowledge about the problems of our own societies is largely bookish, and the books that we read are mainly from the West....We are beggars, all of us—we sneak under many an academic table to gather the crumbs under them. And we mix these bits and make a hash which we pretend to relish, but which we can hardly digest. We have hardly made a contribution to academic cuisine, and have thought it impossible to prepare a dish of our own, with a recipe we have made, using ingredients we have.

Suggesting that an uncritical acceptance of the "traditional social sciences which have been developed as part of the totality of learning in the West" is not desirable, A.C. Espiritu (Philippines) (1968:43) had this to say:

> It is of the highest priority that the teachers and practitioners in the social sciences in Asia emancipate themselves from the value bias of western concepts and postulates of reasoning.... Asian social scientists should undergo a truly creative engagement with their own culture and society, making use, in the process, of frameworks that provide standards of relevance to the experience and aspirations of their own people.

John Samy (Fiji) (1978:30), speaking about the need of Pacific nations boldly asserted:

> We need, amongst other things, a relevant social science with *appropriate* analytical tools, in order to articulate and transform the 'Pacific way' into a reality in this rapidly changing and shrinking world. Quite clearly, this is a task not for any one single person, academic, or discipline, and least, if at all, for foreign social scientists.

In his keynote address to the tenth World Congress of Anthropological and Ethnological Sciences (1978), S.C. Dube (1979:6) castigated Third World anthropologists for not playing a more decisive role of enriching the discipline with the articulation of a grassroots consciousness. He observed:

> Some of the self-proclaimed leaders of the profession in these countries have not been able to decolonize their minds either in respect of theory and method, or in the choice of themes for research and analytical treatment. They have failed to assert their individuality and autonomy. High prestige centres of learning continue to provide them their academic stimulation and models. Their intellectual styles continue to be imitative. The facade of international science hides their interaction only with the select in a charmed circle.... This false notion of internationalism turns them into a highly alienated group. The new consciousness of the Third World can find only a distorted reflection in the products of their prodigious research industry. Their lopsided values result in cultivation of conceptual trivia to the neglect of purposive research on the vital and live issues of the day.... A curious aspect of international social science is that some operators of little academic worth, who are the subject of endless private jokes and a favourite theme of discussion at cocktail parties, can get catapulted to dizzy heights. It is tragic that the Third World should see itself largely through western eyes...And of course, anthropologists of the Third World do not address themselves to the people they study. Writing in a foreign language, they communicate only with their profession.

Another anthropologist, P.L. Bennagen (1979:48) of the Philippines, emphasizes the need

> to smash an anachronistic mirror as a much delayed celebration of the death of old-type colonialism, the decisive historical condition which accelerated the growth of anthropology as a discipline. It is to speak of a new responsibility—that of natives constructing their own mirror to reflect new realities.

Apart from the criticism of the outward-oriented academic elite by the members of that very class which has become increasingly disenchanted by the lure of the West, there is also a demand made by the non-elite in the profession: the less-known practitioners of the discipline, and also the students. Because of their location on the periphery, and because of their lack of competence in communication through an alien language, the larger group of teachers feel deprived and regard themselves victims of the conspiracy of the country's academic elite. Their attitude towards indigenization is less articulate and quite ambivalent. In stronger terms, they ask for literature in the native language; at the same time, they doubt the intentions of the vociferous advocates of indigenization. Aren't these the very people who have reaped the benefits of outside exposure and become part of an international caucus? What have they themselves done to indigenize the social sciences, besides noise-making? Is not the advocacy of indigenization just a posture for keeping the non-elite in the country insulated from the outside, but keeping themselves in the international circuit? Is not the following hidden curriculum of the campaign for indigenization: "Let those who are ignorant of Western social science remain so and thus ill-trained; let us, who know, continue the contact and earn more recognition by assuming a critical posture and performing the role of spokesmen for the underdog?"

It is my feeling that the demand for indigenization is not yet fully regionalized; nor is it possible. It is largely raised in the national and the disciplinary contexts. Countries that are relative latecomers to the social science field are not in a position to make such a demand; the preconditions for it do not exist. They are still in the phase of introducing the social sciences, and they have to depend for it on centres of excellence located elsewhere. Even the change of reference groups from the West to those countries in the region that have a well-developed social science enterprise will not serve the cause of indigenization; after all, they too are outsiders. In the late-comer countries, books, the faculty and other material support are still sought from outside; there has been very little "application" of social sciences to cause dissatisfaction with them. The only demand to emerge is for literature in the national language chosen as the medium of instruction. But even this demand does not exist in the small nations of the Pacific which have opted for an international language as their medium of instruction. The countries that had the advantage of an early start and thus have more than three generations of social scientists are the ones where the call for indigenization has been the strongest, and on several counts: localization, language shift, paradigm replacement, return to native categories of thought, glorification of tradition, and condemnation of foreign academic colonialism.

Proponents of indigenization are aware of the dangers of a mere rhetoric of counter-attack. They do not wish to appear as "courageous natives talking back to alien masters", or as chauvinists. Some of the positive aspects of indigenization being emphasized by its exponents are:

1. Indigenization is a plea for self-awareness and rejection of a borrowed consciousness. It emphasizes the need for an inside view. Its proponents wish to stimulate such scholarly endeavour so as to promote thoughtful analysis of their own societies to replace the existing trend of knowing these via the West.

2. Indigenization advocates the desirability for alternative perspectives on human societies with a view to making the social sciences less parochial and enriching them. This would, it is believed, emancipate the mind and improve the quality of professional praxis, so that society can be examined through new lenses.
3. Indigenization draws attention to historical and cultural specificities and argues for the redefinition of focus, with a view to developing dynamic perspectives on national problems.
4. Indigenization should not lead to narrow parochialism, or to the fragmentation of a single discipline into several insulated systems of thought based on geographical boundaries. It is opposed not only to false universalism but also to false nationalism. Reduced to the level of national narcissism, indigenization would be rendered futile.

In his article, "Indigenization and Transnational Co-operation in the Social Sciences", Krishna Kumar (1979) differentiates between three types of indigenization: structural, substantive and theoretical. To take his definitions: (a) "Structural indigenization can be defined with reference to the institutional and organizational capabilities of a nation for the production and diffusion of social science knowledge" (p. 104); (b) "Substantive indigenization can be conceptualized within the content focus of the social sciences. The essential premise is that the main thrust of these disciplines in a country should be on its own society, people, and economic and political institutions" (p. 104); (c) "Theoretic indigenization indicates a condition in which the social scientists of a nation are involved in constructing distinctive conceptual frameworks and metatheories which reflect their worldviews, social and cultural experience, and perceived goals" (p. 105).

Krishna Kumar does not regard structural and content indigenization as problematic, and dwells at length on the problem of theoretic indigenization and comes to the "right" conclusion that it is not indigenization but "transnational co-operation" that ought to be encouraged (1979:114-16). In doing so, he touches only one aspect of the dilemma. Although relayed in high accent, indigenization invites thinking about a strategy to match the twin concerns of diffusion of a universal social science culture and the need for roots in different cultural settings. It is not without significance that in this debate the word "indigenization" is generally preferred to "endogenous development". Taken literally, endogenous development signifies development generated from within and orthogenetically, which would, thus, have no place for any exogenous influence. In fact, it was in strong reaction to an externally produced and directed strategy of development that the slogan for endogenous development was coined; it is a different matter that so much outside interest continues to pervade endogenous development, making the newer slogan somewhat redundant. Indigenization, by contrast, at least honestly alludes to outside contact by emphasizing the need for indigenizing the exogenous elements to suit local requirements; whether this is done by the "indigenous" or by "outsiders" is a mere detail.

It is also clear from current academic trends that the concern for indigenization is spreading globally. It is not only the countries of the Third World that are talking about indigenization; one can even find articles on "Canadization"! The concern for indigenization among researchers from the developed world is received with a certain pinch of salt. This is how John Samy of Fiji reporting on the discussion on "Theory and Methods" at the recent Young Nations Conference (Mamak and McCall, 1979:242-43) describes a familiar situation:

> The Conference received and entertained a barrage of attractive and emotionally persuasive developmentalist jargon. Some of these words were local products while others were *carefully indigenized to* suit the Pacific taste [italics supplied].

> But even more importantly, much of the talking at the Conference was at cross-purposes, arising from a very sharp dichotomy between foreigners (that is, Australians, New Zealanders and other metropolitan researchers) and the locals (that is, Pacific Islanders, or the researched)...
>
> Most of the so-called foreign or expatriate researchers people. On the other hand, most Pacific Islanders, once they settled down, seemed to enjoy the privilege of being brought to Sydney to advise and guide the foreigners on relevant research.

In the Asian context, indigenization has been pursued along four fronts: (a) teaching in the national language and use of local materials, (b) research by insiders, (c) determination of research priorities, and (d) theoretical and methodological reorientation. A word on each is in order.

Teaching in the National Language and Use of Local Materials

Several countries of the region are taking steps to introduce the national language as the medium of instruction at higher levels of learning; this is a logical second step after the introduction of the national language as a medium of instruction at primary and secondary levels of education. In the case of India, the problem is further compounded by the fact that the constitution recognizes fourteen regional languages, and the various states are moving towards the adoption of regional languages for purposes of instruction. The implications of this policy on the growth of social sciences may be noted.

In those countries where social sciences are a relatively recent implant, most teachers have been trained abroad and do not possess the competence to conduct classes in the national language. In countries with a longer social science tradition, faculties are broadly stratified between the senior professoriate, with linguistic competence in a foreign language only, middle-level faculty members possessing a good command of a foreign language, but also some competence in the national language, and younger faculty members with poor competence in a foreign language but facility in the national language. Such a situation creates a communication crisis. Students are deprived of the training that can only be imparted by senior faculty, and receive instruction only from junior teachers who generally lack experience.

Acceptance of a national language as the medium of instruction requires the production of literature in that language. Most of the books available in non-Asian languages are beyond the comprehension of the majority of students now entering postgraduate departments. As they received their education in the vernacular language, they are at a disadvantage when asked to consult material or listen to lectures in a foreign language. They therefore demand books in the national language. But the demand for books in the vernacular cannot be fulfilled by the seniors who, though experts in the field, lack communication skills in the vernacular. This has given rise to a class of saviours. In terms of their authorship, the books produced in vernacular languages can be classified into the following five categories: (a) books of a tolerable scientific level but poorly written; (b) books whose scientific level is low, written in non-technical language; (c) books that contain a fair balance between language and content; (d) those that are simply bad in content as well as in language; (e) books (very few) that are competently done, most of these being translations. As I have written elsewhere (Atal, 1976:138):

> It must be said that many of the so-called 'original' textbooks are at best examples of plagiarism. The craft of writing a textbook has certain distinguishing features: the subject matter of these books is determined by the university syllabi; considerable distortion is introduced during the process of translation; mostly one foreign book is made the base and a vernacular version is prepared in which footnotes are made a part of the text; the emphasis is laid

> more on definitions and quotations, and less on examples and illustrations from the local setting. Produced cheaply, and in large quantities, these books, like bad money, keep good books out of circulation. Question-answer type essays, 'keys' and 'an hour before the examination' series flood the market and the vulnerable student falls an easy prey to these allurements. The beneficiaries are mainly the publishers; the sufferer is social science. The damage done this way is beyond repair; after a habit of short-cut journeys, a long and circuitous route of hard work cannot attract traffic. The existing system of examination, emphasizing memorizing, has fostered this tendency. Induction into social sciences through such a back door has had a telling effect on the teaching standards. It is the riff-raff social science that is taught and learnt in our colleges. Those centres which have stuck to English or any other foreign language have, in the process, become elite centres; a class-structure has thus emerged in the profession, where the elites are mostly alienated from the cultural context, and the non-elite are ill-prepared to respond to the new challenges.

The new generation of social scientists, because of their lack of competence in an international language, are likely to remain unexposed to the recent developments in the discipline in other countries. Likewise, their own work will not reach foreign researchers and colleagues. Such an insulation will isolate the national social scientists from the world community. The same thing may happen within the country if regional (provincial) languages are made the medium of instruction.

The senior faculty's continuous insistence on a foreign language, disregarding the reality of the switch-over to the national language, has already created a hiatus between faculty and students. The students disapprove of the discrimination against them because of their inability to command a foreign language. They might argue that their lack of competence in the international language cannot be ascribed to them. It was not their fault that they studied in the national language; it was the government's decision. They naively complain that it is the fault of the social science faculty in neglecting the important and ramifying change in the educational system, initiated by the government's language policy. They should have responded to the change and been prepared to meet the new challenge. Students of change have, in a way, failed in their own field of specialization.

Research by Insiders

One significant step towards indigenization taken by most countries is the promotion of research by the "locals", and curbing of "expatriate" research. Several methodological problems concerning research by insiders versus outsiders have come to the fore. It may, however, be maintained that restricting outsiders' research has not always been guided by academic considerations; political considerations have also prevented insiders from doing research on certain themes. Cases can be cited where governments allowed expatriates to carry out research on the most "relevant" areas while insiders were not permitted to do research on those very themes. Curbs on the publication of research findings is yet another problem; while the foreign researchers enjoy relative freedom to collect material and publish the findings, the locals may never be allowed to do so.

The Question of Priorities

One dimension of indigenization is promotion of research on themes regarded as nationally important and relevant. In the developing countries of Asia, this revolution of relevances has pervaded all sectors. In planning activities, and in the allocation of resources, relevance is used as the key criterion. Priorities are attempted in terms of relevance. Both the introduction of social science teaching and the promotion of research are determined in accordance with this criterion.

However, this is not a simple matter. Although everybody seems to agree on the general principle of relevance, it has not been easy to identify its parameters. Not only do these differ from country to country, even within a country, it is hard to reach a consensus on them. Different political platforms provide different sets of priorities for national development. Depending on the nature of "commitment" of social scientists, they may side with one or another political group. The problem is further compounded when research priorities are to be determined for a given social science discipline. The setting up of priorities for a scientific discipline depends on a number of factors, both intrinsic to the discipline and within the external social and political milieu. The existing body of knowledge relative to society, available theoretical tools and methodological apparatus, availability of trained manpower, and an infrastructure of research, are the internal elements of the situation. To these may be added external factors, both social and ideological. Viewed in this light, one can easily locate the potential for value conflict. Thus, in the name of indigenization, different scholarly groups have tried to promote different sets of priorities. There are those who regard only indigenous categories of thought important and consider all imported theories and models irrelevant. There are others who dismiss all the work done so far, either by locals or by foreigners, because it is not in line with their mode of thinking (which may be their own or borrowed). Still others would like social scientists to do committed research and give up all claims to objectivity.

One offshoot of this demand for indigenization has been the undertaking of surveys of existing researches with a view to identifying, on the one hand, the least researched topics and ethnic groups and, on the other, taking an inventory of the theoretical and methodological contributions made by indigenous scholars. A review of such studies can reveal the extent to which indigenization has actually been practised.

Theoretical and Methodological Reorientation

This is happening at a much slower pace. While there is too much iconoclastic talk about the "domination" of alien models and theories and their inappropriateness, there is very little to commend by way of an acceptable alternative. Along with criticism of so-called "capitalist", "status quo" or "Western" social science one may come across those who press the claims of Marxist alternatives. But such alternatives in the name of indigenization are hardly justifiable. By being a "more desirable" perspective, Marxism does not shed its "alien" character and become indigenous. Efforts are still needed to test the alleged universality of established theories and models in a variety of settings. It is not so much an alternative which is really needed if one is to pursue the goal of a universal science—and not the setting up of "schools of thought", like sects, creating a priesthood and a blind following. Genuine efforts, which go beyond reactive rhapsodies, are rare. But some effort is being made. One can cite, as an example, the work of the well-known Pakistani economist, Mahbub Ul Haq, whose collection of essays in *Poverty Curtain* gives clear evidence of reconsideration of basic premises of a development paradigm learnt at Harvard and Yale, and an attempt at reformulation of the strategy in the light of new facts. Though written in a somewhat belligerent style to attract attention and overcome resistance, Haq is constructive in his approach. He finds that the academic community in the Western world which "reacted in shocked disbelief" because "one of its own products had suddenly gone berserk" has now accepted his formulations and premises. More work of this nature is perhaps needed.

Conclusion

The concern shown for indigenization has made it necessary to examine coolly and carefully all its implications. The demand for indigenization is an invitation to re-examine the very structure of social sciences and to evolve suitable strategies for their promotion in the differing and challenging situations of modern times. Although the word has gained considerable currency, there appears to be a lack of consensus on its meaning and desirability.

The thorny dilemma of universality of science and specificities of cultures is the key issue; the demand for deparochialization of Western social sciences perhaps sums up the current social science crisis. One also notices an alarming gap between profession and practice; most of those who have articulated their discontent with Western social science and have advocated indigenization have not given proof of their seriousness by either discarding so-called Western theories, concepts and methods in their work or developing alternative models. The present phase seems still to be one of reaction and resistance. A need exists to distinguish carefully between indigenous and indigenized, between endogenous development and indigenization, and between universalistic and particularistic aspects of indigenization. It must also be recognized that different countries are at different stages of social science development and this determines the extent of their readiness to accept the "ideology" of indigenization. The preconditions for the indigenization of social sciences will have to be identified, for in their absence the call for indigenization will have no real meaning. These preconditions will have to be determined at the individual, professional, institutional, national and regional levels. For this, it may be necessary to take the debate to national, provincial, and local forums of social scientists. Systematic survey of the social science literature generated in the developing countries may provide leads to the attempts made to indigenize disciplines and the problems encountered in such a pursuit.

References

Alatas, Syed Hussein, 1972, "The Captive Mind in Development Studies" in *International Social Science Journal,* Vol. XXIV, No. 1, pp. 9-25.

Atal, Yogesh, 1974, *Social Sciences in Asia,* Abhinav Publications, New Delhi.

Atal, Yogesh, 1976, *Social Sciences: The Indian Scene,* Abhinav Publications, New Delhi.

Bennagen, Ponciano L., 1977, "Mirror, Mirror on the Wall, Are we Human After All?" in A. C. Carlos and A. R. Magno (eds.) *The Social Responsibilities of the Social Scientist as an Intellectual,* Quezon City, Division of Social Sciences, College of Arts and Sciences, University of the Philippines.

Dube, S.C., 1979, "Anthropology and the Challenge of Development" in *Research Bulletin,* Vol. 1, No. 2, pp. 4-8, Association of Third World Anthropologists, Williamsburg.

Espiritu, A. Cesar, 1968, "The Limits of Applicability of Western Concepts, Values and Methods in the Social Sciences to the Concrete Realities of Asian Societies" in *The Relevance of the Social Sciences in Contemporary Asia,* World Student Christian Federation, Tokyo.

Haq, Mahbub Ul, 1976, *The Poverty Curtain: Choices for the Third World,* Columbia University Press, New York.

Kumar, Krishna (ed.), 1979, *Bonds Without Bondage,* East-West Cultural Learning Institute, Honolulu.

Kumar, Krishna (ed.), 1979, "Indigenization and Transnational Cooperation in the Social Sciences" in *Bonds Without Bondage,* East-West Cultural Learning Institute, Honolulu.

Kurien, Christopher T., 1968, "Planning in Asian Countries: A Critique" in *The Relevance of the Social Sciences in Contemporary Asia,* World Student Christian Federation, Tokyo.

Kwon, T'ae-Hwan, 1979, Seminar on Koreanizing Western Approaches to Social Sciences, *Korea Journal,* Vol. 19, No. I 1, pp. 20-25.

Mamak, Alexandar; McCall, Grant (eds.), 1978, *Paradise Postponed: Essays on Research and Development in the South Pacific,* Pergamon Press, Rushcutters Bay, NSW.

Samy, John, 1978, "Development and Research for Whom? Towards a Critique of Economism in the Pacific, and Session on Theory and Methods" in Alexandra Mamak and Grant McCall (eds.) *Paradise Postponed: Essays on Research and Development in the South Pacific*, Pergamon Press, Rushcutters Bay, NSW.

UNESCO, 1977, *Inter-Regional Co-operation in the Social Sciences* UNESCO (Reports and Papers in the Social Sciences, 36.), Paris.

Yamaoka, Kikuo, 1968, "Introduction" in *The Relevance of the Social Sciences in Contemporary Asia*, World Student Christian Federation, Tokyo.

6

Indigenization: The Case of Indian Sociology[*]

The earlier phases of the post-colonial Third World were characterized by the simultaneous operation of two processes, viz., of decolonization and development. With the departure of the colonial powers, the newly emergent nations engaged in the exercise of nation building in terms of demolishing the colonial structures of administration, freeing the "captive mind" (a phrase coined by S.H. Alatas, 1972), and initiating a process of development—economic, political, and even social and cultural. The charisma of independence overwhelmed everyone in those societies, and the desire to catch up with the developed world in every respect reigned supreme. Decolonization, in such a context, meant developing a distance from the former colonizer culture and creation of a distinct national identity. In both these efforts, the emergent nations took two apparently opposite steps—that of "looking inward" to revive and energize traditional culture, and to establish new reference groups in the outer world away from the colonizer country. The desire was at once to relate to the wider outside world and to reinforce the moorings in the native soil.

I characterize the colonial situation as a *single-aperture model.* The colonized societies were exposed to the outside

---

* Reprinted from *IASSI Quarterly*, Vol. 18, No.3, 2000, pp. 28-44.

world—particularly the Western world—mainly via the colonizer country. Only that country served as the reference group; the language, the education system, the way of life, and even the mode of thinking of the people in the colonies were influenced by the culture of the colonizer. This was replaced by the *multiple-aperture model* in the post-colonial period when newly independent countries began to look at different countries for ideas and inspirations. It became multiple also in the sense that people began to open their doors to their own past. Insulations that separated the people from their past and from the rest of the world thus began to crumble.

The euphoria of independence gradually began to die with the realistic assessments of the gains and losses in the emergent situation. Already in the 1950s, some scholars were able to highlight a trend reversal: the so-called "rising revolution of aspirations" was giving way to the "rising revolution of frustrations". There ensued a process of disenchantment with the prevailing paradigm of development. New forms of "dependencies" were noticed in the economic and political field. And concerns were being shown to the growth of a newer form of "academic colonialism" emanating from another source—USA or USSR. It was felt that the pattern of vertical relationship between the scholars of the Third World and the scholars from the "donor" countries had not ended with the attainment of political freedom. Young and bright students and lecturers from the developing countries were lured to the academic metropolises; their return after an exposure to the intellectual milieu of these countries ensured that these would become the advocates of their line of reasoning. Such people became the pioneers in their respective countries initiating new courses or changing the syllabi. They were designated as "captive minds" by some indigenous scholars, but treated by their mentors in the Western academe as carriers of modernization to their respective parent cultures. The need was felt then to change both the development paradigm and the orientation of social sciences. It is in that context that I wrote: "Development strategists are sloganizing the need for endogenous development; social scientists are agonising about indigenization" (Atal, 1981:189).

There was almost a worldwide clamour for the indigenization of social sciences in the 1970s. Of course, the call for indigenization came from the social scientists of the developing countries who raised their voice against "implantation of social sciences". But it is interesting to note that even the Conference of National Social Science Councils and analogous bodies (CNSSC)—which later became International Federation of Social Science Organizations (IFSSO)—took up this issue for discussion in 1977. It is important to mention here that while IFSSO is international, it is largely an organization of the "developed" world. Around the same time, the East-West Centre of the University of Hawaii got interested in this issue. America's Wenner-Gren Foundation also organized, in 1978, a conference on indigenous anthropology. Even Canadian social scientists held a symposium on Canadization of social sciences, not to talk of Korean initiative on Koreanization of social sciences.

American interest in indigenization had, however, a different orientation. Since much of the American social science was "American", it was already "indigenous" for them. The crisis for them was not to indigenize social sciences but to ensure their universalization through their spread in other intellectual traditions. The call for indigenization appeared to them as a threat to the Western social science—that it will restrict its spread, and that this may mean difficulties for the Western social scientists in getting clearance from the host governments to carry out field research. From this angle, the demand for indigenization by the social scientists of the developing countries was seen almost as an affront to the American social science. It is interesting that the advocates of indigenization somehow spared the Marxist approach from their criticism; the campaign for indigenization appeared as a campaign against capitalistic social science.

The etiology of indigenization is quite complicated, so is its definition. Concerns were shown for lack of autonomy and individuality in the choice of themes, or use of theory and methods, and imitative character of the emerging Third World social science. There were criticisms of "cultivation of conceptual trivia", of writing in a foreign language as if to communicate only with their professional peers abroad and not sharing their research findings with the common man of their own society. An Indian economist, with a Marxist inclination wrote in his characteristic style: "We have hardly made a contribution to academic cuisine, and have thought it impossible to prepare a dish of our own, with a recipe we have made, using ingredients we have" (Kurien, 1968:17-18). Advocates of indigenization had different emphases: localization (replacement of foreign faculty by the local), language shift from the foreign language to the mother-tongue, paradigm replacement, return to the native categories of thought, non-applicability of Western research techniques and methods, and overall condemnation of the foreign academic colonialism. For some, indigenization meant glorification of tradition, and return to the corridors of the past reducing the demand to some sort of national narcissism.

Reviewing these trends in 1981, I outlined the following features of the call for indigenization:

1. Indigenization is a plea for self-awareness and rejection of a borrowed consciousness. It emphasizes the need for an inside view. Its proponents wish to stimulate such scholarly endeavour so as to promote thoughtful analysis of their own societies to replace the existing trend of knowing these via the West.

2. Indigenization advocates the desirability for alternative perspectives on human societies with a view to making the social sciences less parochial and enriching them. This would, it is

believed, emancipate the mind and improve the quality of professional praxis, so that society can be examined through new lenses.

3. Indigenization draws attention to historical and cultural specificities and argues for the redefinition of focus, with a view to developing dynamic perspectives on national problems.

4. Indigenization should not lead to narrow parochialism, or to the fragmentation of a single definition into several insulated systems of thought based on geographical boundaries. It is opposed not only to false universalism but also to false nationalism. Reduced to the level of national narcissism, indigenization would be rendered futile [Atal, 1981:192-3].

Indigenization in the 1980s, it must be said, was still largely in its reactive phase in the sense that much of the debate was couched as a reaction to the introduction, or implantation, of Western social science. There was very little to demonstrate either an indigenized product theory or methodology, or an indigenous social science. Let it be said that the difference between the two is important. The word indigenization connotes the process of indigenizing something that is exogenous whereas indigenous refers to something that has originated from within. Replacement of exogenous categories of thought by the indigenous ones was also regarded as a part of the process of indigenization.

The Case of Indian Sociology

Sociology in India has a long history. It is significant that sociology in India is much older than in Australia and New Zealand despite the fact that they were also colonies of the British.[1] The oldest department of sociology at the Bombay University celebrated its platinum jubilee in 1995. The tradition of research into the peoples and cultures of India is even older. But these anthropological studies were carried out by the Westerners, mainly Britishers.[2] While talking about sociology in India it may be useful to keep in mind both the aspects, namely sociological (and anthropological) studies of Indian society, and teaching of these subjects in India. It is from this angle that it can be said that while the teaching of these subjects in India is relatively recent compared to other social and human sciences, researches on Indian society have a longer past. This distinction also impresses the other point that most of the earlier studies on the cultures and society of India were carried out by "outsiders"; researches by "insiders" are a later phenomenon which mostly coincides with the introduction of these subjects in the curricula of Indian universities. However, it is also significant that the first generation teachers were either trained abroad in these disciplines, or moved from other sister disciplines.

"Initially, the British were interested in the life of the people only to the extent such knowledge served to help them in their trade. After they assumed political power, however, they faced different problems" (Desai, 1981: 11). Way back in 1858, following a proclamation by Queen Victoria to the effect that the Hindus and Muslims will be governed by their own laws, the British set up in Calcutta a college for Indian studies. Through direct observations and examination of the written records of the past, the British attempted to understand the Indian society, giving birth to, what came to be known as, indological studies. Reviewing the literature of those times, I.P. Desai made three conclusions: "(i) social studies [Desai perhaps meant social sciences, but felt hesitant to call those studies by this name.] grew as a part of indological studies; (ii) they were predominantly evaluatory; (iii) they were not divorced from practical problems"(Ibid.: 13). The interpretations offered by the British writers to indological texts were viewed differently by different native scholars depending upon their attitude towards the British. Desai has classified these reactions into three categories:

1. acceptance of the way of life of the impacting society and perhaps contempt for the indigenous way of life;

2. complete rejection of the way of life of the impacting society with complete acceptance of the indigenous way of life; and

3. acceptance as a fact of the impact of an alien society and the consequent changes in native society, side by side with recognition of India's past and its efficacy [Ibid.: 14].

It is in such a climate that teaching of sociology and anthropology in the Indian universities began with the inclusion of this subject in the courses of other disciplines.

An urban planner with a degree in geography, from New Zealand—Sir Patrick Geddes—came to start the department of sociology at the Bombay University in 1919. He selected G.S. Ghurye—then a lecturer in Sanskrit at the Elphinston College in Bombay—to go to England to learn sociology at Cambridge under W.H.R. Rivers—an anthropologist. Another appointee, N.A. Thoothi, got his training at Oxford under R.R. Merret, J.L. Myers and J. Arthur Thomson—again all anthropologists. Upon their return, these "sociologists" taught courses on caste and rank, marriage and family, archaeology and world prehistory [no sociologist today will claim specialization in this field in India, other than some anthropologists-turned-sociologists like me who also taught archaeology and physical anthropology and palaeontology in their formative years.] I.P. Desai who was a student of Ghurye and Thoothi in the 1930s says that in his student days: "(1) methodology as a separate course was not learnt by any of the sociologists; (2) sociology was not understood as a science as it is understood today; and (3) sociology was supposed to have a bearing on practical life and was future oriented, that is, change oriented" (Ibid.:20). Desai does not regard the earlier preoccupations of the founding fathers as "unsociological" judging them from what is expected today of the sociologists. He forcefully argues: "Ghurye went to Sindh and Saurashtra and himself did the digging to find the spread of Buddhistic and Mohen-jo-daro culture not because he was not a sociologist, but because he was a sociologist as understood in those days. It is also not surprising that Aiyappan (an anthropologist) became the curator of Madras Museum. D.N. Majumdar's (another anthropologist who began his career as lecturer in the department of economics at the Lucknow University) interest in Himalayan expeditions and anthropometry was not career oriented, but was consistent with the theory and practice of his discipline of the time" (Ibid.: 41).

Sociology and anthropology entered the Lucknow University via the department of economics that had stalwarts like Radha Kamal Mukerjee and D.P. Mukerji. While the scholarship at Bombay was trying to establish a distinct identity for sociology vis-à-vis Indology, the Lucknow pioneers had to carve out a separate niche for the new disciplines out of economics. Here, one finds emphasis on the logico-philosophical approach and even introduction of Marxism. Interestingly, in their attempt to establish a separate identity for Indian sociology, the Lucknow scholars advocated for a closer link with Indology. Since the university decided to set up two separate departments for sociology and anthropology, unlike in Bombay, Lucknow also generated debate regarding the distinction between the two disciplines, which started their career in the university from the department of economics. The first generation sociologists from this university had their Master's degrees in economics. D.N. Majumdar—an anthropology graduate from Calcutta with further training from England—was appointed in the department of economics as a "Lecturer in Primitive Economics"!! When new departments of sociology were opened in other universities their bureaucracies found it difficult to consider the applications of economics graduates from the Lucknow University for sociology positions. Later, it also became part of academic politics in the country.

Thus, the people associated with Lucknow led the debate about the nature of Indian sociology and the distinction between sociology and anthropology. The Bombay school did not make any issue, particularly in the beginning, of the relationship between sociology and anthropology. It is interesting that M.N. Srinivas and I.P. Desai—both students of Ghurye came to be identified as representing anthropology and sociology respectively but both worked in the same department of sociology at Baroda. "That there was M.N. Srinivas, a social anthropologist, as head of the department did not come in my way of buying American books for the library and teaching them. The M.A. student was conversant with both American sociology and British sociology or social anthropology. I found it very fruitful to have another teacher with a different sociological outlook in the department" (Desai, 1981:33). Desai further says: "I must make it clear that anthropologists and sociologists were never understood as two 'castes' as they are understood today....Sociology and anthropology had a common theoretical outlook, namely evolutionism. In fact, sociology was something amorphous at least as it was practised then in India and probably elsewhere too. There were no books on sociological theory as such. The books available to us were the books on the history of 'theories'. The two books which I read were Lowie's *History of Ethnological Theories* [1937] and Hadden's *History of Anthropology* [1949]" (Ibid.:46). Desai is of the view that "there was no intellectual or academic ground for the separation of anthropology and sociology" (Ibid.). Both Ghurye—who chaired the first department of sociology in the country—and K.P. Chattopadhyay—who chaired the first department of anthropology in Calcutta—were students of the same professor—W.H.R. Rivers.

The arrival of M.N. Srinivas on the scene, however, made the difference. Desai got the impression from his interaction with him that Srinivas regarded anthropology as "true or real sociology" although both used the same terminology. While questioning the suitability of the quantitative methods and survey research Srinivas emphasized empirical research and anthropological field work and regarded all such work as sociological, and worked hard to differentiate it from indological on the one hand, and social work, on the other. The generation of Srinivas and Desai, from the Bombay school, was thus engaged in providing a distinct identity to sociology and to define in terms of a study of the contemporary Indian society through systematic fieldwork with little emphasis on the so-called theory or conceptual frameworks. Although no one disputed Srinivas' brand of sociology, which continues to flourish at the Delhi University where Srinivas moved from Baroda in the late 1950s, somehow people in the profession identified Desai more with sociology and Srinivas with social anthropology.

Once the twin disciplines took roots in India—sociology more rapidly than social anthropology, particularly in terms of the number of departments—the professionals addressed themselves to the identity crisis. At once, the practitioners of the two disciplines had to work on several fronts:

- To evaluate the writings of the foreign scholars on India.
- To distinguish sociology from Indology and from social anthropology.
- To formally define the scope of Indian sociology and to set the priorities for research.

Questions surrounding these three key concerns have provided the impetus to the call for indigenization. Almost as part of a nationalist agenda the Indian scholarship of the 1940s and 1950s critically reviewed the alien writings on India to detect "colonial designs" and "Western conspiracy" to downgrade Indian culture and civilization as if to prove the superiority of the West. The theories of unilinear evolution, Marxism, structural-functionalism were all seen as part of the Western agenda to maintain an unequal, vertical relationship. In methodological terms, questions were raised regarding the applicability of the Western techniques of research, and also the limitations of an "outsider" to understand the internal structures of relationships. The insider-outsider controversy became a real methodological issue. A special twist to this problem came in anthropology which is defined as the study of "other cultures". The entire discipline's strength is its ability to investigate the cultures to which the anthropologist does not belong. And with the technique of "participant observation" he is able to provide a dependable and "scientific" ethnographic account of a primitive tribe. If one accepts the criticism that the outsider cannot understand an alien culture then all the anthropological researches will have to be discarded. Moreover, there is also a counter view that by simply being an "insider", one cannot claim to have a fuller and better, and accurate understanding of the social phenomena. A further complication is created in the case of Indian anthropologists who have, unlike their Western counterparts, mostly studied Indian society and its subcultures—"how are these 'other' societies for them?" is the question asked. Even when Indians went to study anthropology in England they were sent back to India for fieldwork. Thus while the Indian society remained the "other society" for the foreign mentors of Indian anthropologists, it was not so for the latter. They thus studied them as insiders, violating the defining principle of their discipline. Defending the practice, leading Indian anthropologists regarded the distinction between sociology and social anthropology as rather superfluous. Of course, there were, and perhaps are even now, some in the anthropology profession who advocate a separate calling, and maintain closer links between social anthropology, prehistory and archaeology, and physical anthropology and palaeontology, with insistence on the study of tribal cultures only.

Sociologists also engaged in an exercise to dissociate their subject from indology on the one hand, and social anthropology, on the other. On both fronts, the key distinction was located in the methodology. Indology was regarded as the study of the past and anthropology as the study of the "primitive" by those sociologists who wanted to emphasize on the study of the contemporary society with the use of survey research and quantitative techniques. Indology was held responsible for the "book view" and the "upper caste view" of Indian society that was very different from what the present-day Indian society is. And since anthropology focussed on the tribal societies, it was considered ill-equipped to study and analyze contemporary Indian society. But in the 1950s, with heavy emphasis in Indian planning on agriculture and rural development, and with the inauguration of the Community Development Programme on a massive scale, both sociologists and anthropologists began studying rural India. The village in India became the meeting ground for the twin disciplines. But here again, anthropologists continued the use of the ethnographic method while sociologists followed the survey method to distinguish themselves giving rise to a continued debate in the 1950s and 1960s regarding the status of these disciplines, and questioning the credentials of scholars in terms of whether they are sociologists or anthropologists.[3]

In an attempt to provide a separate identity to sociology, Professor D.P. Mukerji of Lucknow—an economist-turned-sociologist—argued that economics has neglected the social base and, therefore, has provided only "arid abstractions". Although a late-comer, he regarded sociology as a mother of all other social sciences. He began his presidential address to the First All India Sociological Conference, held in 1955 in Dehradun, by acknowledging: "Sociology has a floor and a ceiling, like any other science, but its specialty consists in its floor being the ground-floor of all types of social disciplines, and its ceiling remaining open to the sky" (Mukerji, 1961:20). While endorsing the view that any social science should be engaged in the search for "some basic, neutral and lowest common multiple concepts;...some common methodological principles derived from modern refinements of logic; reorientations and ways of inter-relations, or cross-breeding; and a philosophical approach" (Ibid.). DP (as he was affectionately called by his peers and students) believed that the "...first task for us...is to study the social traditions to which we have been born and in which we had our being. This task includes the study of the changes in traditions by internal and external pressures" (Ibid.:22). For him, indigenization meant study of Indian themes and by Indians, for he believed that

> ...participation by long conditioning, which is the first requisite of understanding, should make it less possible to pass on the most jejune and vapid generalizations about Indian problems with which we are being familiarized today in the name of scientific research. I do not in the least suggest that foreign scholars should be barred from studying Indian problems, but I am only referring to the greater ease of insight and understanding that can be secured by the sociologist when he is saturated in his own traditions (Ibid.:23).

He justifies his position and makes the following prescription for an Indian sociologist:

> His capacity to judge is a matter of acquired discipline, but in the matter of understanding, empathy precedes sympathy. Thus, it is not enough for the Indian sociologist to be a sociologist. He must be an Indian first, that is, he is to share in the folkways, mores, customs, and traditions, for the purpose of understanding his social system and what lies beneath it and beyond it. He should be steeped in Indian lore, both high and low (Ibid.).

Mukerji talked not only of Indian themes, and Indian origin of sociologists as a prerequisite for doing Indian sociology, he also advocated for an Indian brand of technical skill. Thus, he said: "Unless sociological training in India is grounded on Sanskrit, or any such language in which the traditions have been embodied as symbols, social research in India will be a pale imitation of what others are doing. It pains me to observe how our Indian scholars succumb to the lure of modern 'scientific' techniques imported from outside as a part of technical aid and 'know-how', without resistance and dignity. In the intellectual transactions which are taking place, it seems that we have no terms to offer, no ground to stand upon" (Ibid.). Mukerji regarded "all our *shastras* as sociological", and wanted a different paradigm for Indian sociology that would treat "man" as a *Purush*, and not as an "individual" (*Vyakti)* as in the West. This implies that the unit of analysis for Indian sociology will have to be "group" and not an individual. Moreover, "if you are an Indian, and additionally an Indian sociologist" there is "no escape from tradition" (Ibid.: 25). He described traditions as "forgotten facts" and wanted them to be the subject matter of Indian sociology.

Several of DP's students repeated this emphasis in their advocacy for a distinct Indian sociology. Of these, two—R.N. Saksena and A.K. Saran—are taken here as representative examples. First as Principal of the DAV College, Dehradun and then as Director of the newly established Institute of Social Sciences, Saksena contributed a great deal to popularize and spread teaching of sociology in India. He was also the key force behind the organization of All-India Sociological Conferences, hosting the first Conference in Dehradun (1955), and the third in Agra (1958). He presided over the fourth conference held in Calcutta in 1959.[4]

What Saksena said in his Presidential Address in Calcutta has been repeated by him verbatim in several other speeches, but one finds little evidence in his own research writings of the pursuit of that line of enquiry. However, it will be useful to briefly allude to his position regarding the desired character of Indian sociology.

Arguing that "Indian sociologists have inherited a different philosophy" Saksena makes out a case for a different brand of sociology which examines "the relation of man not simply as a relation to other human beings but to all life" (Saksena, 1961:7). Like his teacher DP he also suggests that the analysis of Indian society will have to be in terms of spiritual values which are "...to us not so much a form of mystic religion as a mode of life" (Ibid.:8). He assigns a very important role to religion suggesting that it is around religion that "the whole of Indian social life rotates". He alludes to "traditional sociological thought" and even to Mahatma Gandhi as a product of cultural synthesis. Impressed by the continuity of Indian society, he finds the strength in the vitality of Indian culture. The question that he asks is: "How has India managed to remain more or less the same in the midst of social migrations, upheavals, and political changes that have elsewhere changed the face of society?" (Ibid.:8).

A more rigourous and forceful proponent of an indigenous view of sociology is A.K. Saran, also a product of Lucknow. Saran had taken almost an extreme position by declaring that "sociological cognition and world-view is fundamentally alien to the Indian tradition, hence any attempt towards its indigenization or adaptation into an *Indian* cognitive system is bound either to fail or to turn imitative" (Singh, 1986:6). Saran rejects the idea of a universalistic sociology. He explicated his stand while critically reviewing the stand taken by Louis Dumont and David Pocock *For a Sociology of India* in the inaugural issues of the *Contributions to Indian Sociology* edited by them. Their article generated lot of debate and all those articles published both in the *Contributions* and elsewhere by Indian scholars provide good material on Indian thinking on indigenization. That there are various viewpoints suggests that there is no consensus on either the concept or the desirability of it. The most vocal critic of Western sociology, A.K. Saran has attracted the attention of many but did not find any takers. Nor was he able to demonstrate through concrete studies an alternative mode of sociological research.

Saran chose to advance his argument against the Western brand of sociology as unsuited to unravel the Indian reality by questioning the approach advocated by Dumont and Pocock. First, he argued that an approach suited for the study of the primitive society cannot be replicated for the study of Indian villages and the peasant society by saying "the monographic-ethnographic method" is not applicable to "quasi-traditional (or tradition-haunted) societies" (1962:15). According to him, while the editors of *Contributions* "think of the unity of India in terms of a system of ideas and values, they believe in a seriously misleading method for its study and understanding" (Ibid.). Referring to Parsons' theory of pattern variables—which is utilized by Dumont in his analysis of the Hindu concept of *Trivarga*—Saran says that it "is a logical mongrel, and hence its claim to generality is unfounded. It is merely a lay, informal systematization of the confusions and dilemmas of modern 'society' " (Ibid.:59). He even argues that "highly formalized and technical language" of the Sanskrit texts "cannot be translated in a less formal language. At all events, only distortion can result when it is translated into any other language without a logically rigourous demonstration that one language *as a whole* is reducible to (or isomorphic with) the other" (Ibid.). Summing up his long critique of Dumont and Pocock, Saran makes a general comment about the differing orientations:

> If one insists on the "language" of individualism, it may be said that the West's problem is that of becoming an individual while being in the society, while the Indian problem is to get out of individuality and yet accept Life-in-Society which requires responsible individuals. It is certainly not between two modes of becoming an individual. But our main point has been to show that individuality is not the best concept for the understanding of Indian Society. The central problem of the Indian (traditional) Society arises from the encounter of the Divine and the Human. The task for this society is to keep alive the transcendent, the

> Eternal, through the temporal-social. The central problem of the modern West is: How to maintain social life without a Divine Center [Ibid.:68].

Saran concludes his essay by saying: "...social reality *qua* social has no 'outside'; that the only outside is its interpretation in terms of an alien culture, and that understanding is not furthered but obscured by taking, in the name of science, modernity, or objectivity, a firmly provincial standpoint for the study of traditional or tradition-haunted societies" (Ibid.).

It is evident from this small sample of views of those who had advocated for a different brand of sociology for India that they regarded sociology as a cultural critique or a "reformative ratiocination". They also believed that Indian reality could not be interpreted through an evolutionary perspective that puts societies of the West on a higher pedestal. They found the sociological categories of the West to be too parochial to be applicable to the Indian situation; in other words, inherent in their criticism of the Western theories was the point that these are not theories with universal applicability.

The question of indigenization or Indianization of sociology emerged in the country with its growing professionalization. It is significant that the issue was raised in the first four all-India conferences in the presidential addresses. This was also the time when large number of American and other foreign social scientists began coming to India for carrying out field researches on development-related themes—a situation different from the colonial times when only the anthropologists were coming to study the tribal cultures. In the new setting, the shift of anthropological researches from the tribal societies to the village communities, and the presence of large-scale foreign-funded research projects made many in the profession to ponder over these questions related to the professionalization of sociology in particular, and social sciences in general.

The opinion on the issue of Indian sociology was divided in two polar camps. There were those, like Saran, who would think of a distinct sociology with no connection with the West, and the other extreme was that sociology, as a discipline, cannot be divided into national boundaries and its practitioners must work for developing universal theories. The main criticism of those holding views of a distinct Indian sociology was that they equated India with Hindu India, and even there they failed to make any distinction between the Great Tradition of the literati and the several Little Traditions. Moreover, they failed to acknowledge the polytheistic character of Hinduism as a religion, and the heterogeneity of its various schools of thought. How could a multi-cultural society like that of India be understood only through the "forgotten" traditions? It is too much to regard the classical texts of Hinduism as sociological texts, particularly when most of them are prescriptive in character. Sociological theories are derived from the analyses of well-described lived-in realities—the actually existing social realities—and not the prescriptive codes. A science devoted to the analysis of "was" and "is" is different from a text that speaks the language of the "should" and "must". These texts may be sociologically relevant, but they themselves cannot be regarded as sociological. Doing so would be anachronism.

Different views prevail in regard to the interpretation of the word Indian sociology. There are some who suggest that "Indian sociology is what *Indian* sociologists do". If what is prescribed by the likes of Saran and Saksena is not practised by those who are labelled sociologists then it should be interpreted as rejection of a prescription rather than a dereliction of duty. This definition will also bring into the scope of Indian sociology all work done by Indian sociologists in other societies and cultures. As a corollary, others suggest that Indian sociology consists of the total corpus of work on India irrespective of the nationality of the scholar, Indian or otherwise. Both these views do not disregard the importance of examining the "universality" claims of any given theory or applicability of any research method or technique. They also constructively see the prospects of Indians, or Indian studies, contributing to the general body of theory, or the repertory of social science concepts and methodology. Such practitioners, I am one among them, feel that there is a need to "deparochialise" our theories—be they Western or Oriental—so that they could compete for a universal status.

In the present milieu, the debate regarding indigenization seems to have mellowed down. Not much is heard about it in professional fora, nor is much written about it. However, one finds that increasingly more and more natives are getting involved in teaching and research and increasing attention is being paid to the problems of contemporary concern. In doing so, scholars have tried to employ local/native concepts to explain a situation where a foreign concept has failed to capture the essence. Some have even proposed their own concepts in an international language for the phenomena that are not peculiar to India alone. Such concepts are gaining international currency. It seems that indigenization demand as an expression of nationalism, and an argument for the uniqueness of one's own culture that defies any scientific treatment is a thing of the past. But in the work of the actively engaged sociologists one can find constructive contributions to theory and methodology emanating from the study of their own societies to establish a distinct identity of Indian sociology. Analyzing the contributions to the debate on sociology for India, Yogendra Singh "...finds substantial continuity of concerns...specially on the issue of indigenization of Indian sociology. Yet, one also witnesses in these debates the emergence of new perspectives...The focus shifts from a debate on sociological colonialism or dependency to the constructive formulation and investigation of grounds on which the specific cognitive structure of Indian sociology could be constituted...These viewpoints mark a departure from the early concern with the problem of sociology's indigenization. Not that this problem is not debated during the 1970s and 1980s, but in most cases, indigenization is now identified with an emphasis on historicity, conceptual relevance, and sensitivity to the distinction of levels (regional, national, and cross-national) in attempts to make generalizations through theoretical abstractions in Indian sociology" (Singh, 1986:24).

The new directions that Indian sociology is taking are beautifully summarized by Yogendra Singh. It will be useful to end this essay with a quote by him:

> Despite the continuity reflected in the quest for social relevance and an indigenous paradigm for sociology, the 1970s and 1980s in India mark several directions in which new explorations have been made. First, sociological studies show a new sensitivity in the choice of concepts and their uses as they move away from a continuum framework of analysis of social process to that of a notion of levels. The use of conceptual typologies, historical data and linguistic or symbolic structural techniques adds new depth and dimension to the studies of social structure. The Marxist historical method of analysis gains momentum as a series of studies on the peasantry, agrarian structure, and working classes gains ground. Instead of preoccupation with the ritual aspects of caste and its cultural and social functions, or with simplistic dichotomization between caste and class, new series of studies sensitive to theoretical orientations such as structuralism, ethnosociology, systems analysis and historical materialist methods of Marxism and neo-Marxism have been conducted to analyse the social structure both in specific regional and macroscopic national settings. Such studies tend to be more analytic and to aim at explanation rather than mere description, so common in the sociological tradition of the 1950s [Singh, 1986: 25-6].

Notes

1. It is important to mention that Oxford still does not have a department of sociology, and that Cambridge started the department of sociology as late as 1968. Ethnology was, of course, defined as "Comparative Sociology".
2. Anthropology's colonial linkage is still decried by many who feel that these studies were primarily meant to understand the native societies and cultures and to educate the colonial administrators so that the colonial grip remains stronger.
3. I remember one instance where in a conference the chairman of the session congratulated me for making a "good sociological" remark, but was later disappointed to learn that I was an anthropologist. So I said, "How does it matter?" He said there is great difference between the two disciplines, one starts with "S" and the other with "A". "But", I retorted, "Professor, both end with "Y". He did not appreciate the pun and left.
4. It must be said here that these conferences, though called All-India, were an effort to create an association of the scholars who had connections with the Lucknow school. People connected with Bombay became members of the Indian Sociological Society. Quite interestingly, the character of the All-India Sociological Conferences was interdisciplinary as it had sessions on sociology, anthropology, and social psychology. All the Presidents of the first four conferences were from Lucknow; besides DP and R.N. Saksena, who presided the Dehradun and Calcutta sessions respectively, D.N. Majumdar (anthropologist) presided over the Patna session (1957), and Radhakamal Mukerjee (economist turned sociologist) chaired the Agra conference (1958). Later, the conference was amalgamated with the Indian Sociological Society which agreed to own even the previous conferences that were not held under its auspices.

References

Alatas, Syed Hussein, 1972, "The Captive Mind in Development Studies" in *International Social Science Journal*, Vol. XXIV, No. 1, pp. 9 25.

Atal, Yogesh, 1971, "Professionalization of Sociologists", *Economic and Political Weekly*, VI (6), pp. 431-33.

—, 1976, *Social Sciences: The Indian Scene*, Abhinav Publications, New Delhi.

—, 1981, "The Call for Indigenization", *International Social Science Journal*, Vol. XXXIII, No. 1, pp. 189-97.

— (ed.), 1985, *Sociology and Social Anthropology in Asia and the Pacific*, Wiley Eastern, New Delhi and UNESCO, Paris.

Desai, I.P., 1981, *The Craft of Sociology and Other Essays*, Ajanta Publications, Delhi.

Dube, S.C., 1979, "Anthropology and the Challenge of Development, *Research Bulletin*, Vol. 1, No. 2, pp. 4-8, Association of Third World Anthropologists, Williamsburg.

Kumar, Krishna (ed.), 1979, *Bonds Without Bondage*, East-West Cultural Learning Institute, Honolulu.

Kurien, Christopher T., 1968, "Planning in Asian Countries: A Critique", in *The Relevance of the Social Sciences in Contemporary Asia*, World Student Christian Federation, Tokyo.

Kwon, T'ae-Hwan, 1979, "Seminar on Koreanizing Western Approaches to Social Sciences", *Korea Journal*, Vol. 19, No. 1, pp. 20-25.

Mukerjee, Radhakamal, 1961, "A Philosophy of Social Science" in Saksena (ed.), *Sociology, Social Research and Social Problems in India*, Asia Publishing House, Bombay.

Mukerji, D.P., 1961, "Indian Sociology and Tradition" in Saksena (ed.), *Sociology, Social Research and Social Problems in India*, Asia Publishing House, Bombay.

Mukherjee, Ramkrishna, 1979, *Sociology of Indian Sociology*, Allied Publishers, Bombay.

Saberwal, Satish, 1983, "For a Sociology of India - Uncertain Transplants: Anthropology and Sociology in India", *Contributions to Indian Sociology* (new series), Vol. 17, No.2, pp.301-16.

Saksena, R.N. (ed.), 1961, *Sociology, Social Research and Social Problems in India*, Asia Publishing House, Bombay.

Saran, A.K., 1962, "Review of Contributions to Indian Sociology", No. IV (April 1959), *The Eastern Anthropologist*. Vol.XV. No. 1, pp.53-68.

Sharma, Surendra, 1985, *Sociology in India: A Perspective from Sociology of Knowledge*, Rawat Publications, Jaipur.

Singh, Yogendra, 1986, *Indian Sociology: Social Conditioning and Emerging Concerns*, Vistaar Publications, New Delhi.

UNESCO, 1977, *Inter-Regional Co-operation in the Social Sciences*, UNESCO (Reports and Papers in the Social Sciences, 36.), Paris.

7

Social Sciences: Use for Policy*

I

Three important processes characterize the knowledge industry: creation, diffusion, and utilization. Over the years, more social science knowledge in India has been *created* through research, and *diffused* through teaching, but there are complaints of its relative *non-utilization* by policy makers and planners. It is in this connection that questions of *relevance* are raised and the need for *commitment* is emphasized.

It must be recognized that there has been a remarkable burst of activity in the social sciences in the last few decades, particularly after the country became independent. The size of the social science community has grown, the volume of social science publication has increased manifold, and the demand for social science expertise has risen. Not only is the social scientist needed for the performance of conventional roles within the precincts of an academic institution, he is also called upon to assist the business enterprises, healthcare units, government bureaus, and above all, the national planning agency in one of the several capacities such as researcher, adviser, consultant, administrator and planner. Such an expansion of the range of activities of the social scientists notwithstanding, there persists a

---

* Reprinted from *International Social Science Journal*, Vol. XXXV, No. 2, 1983 under the title "Using the Social Sciences for Policy Formulation", pp. 367-77.

general feeling that research is not sufficiently related to government policy, and that social scientists are not accorded the respect that they deserve. A gap seems to exist between the producers of research and its consumers. The question of utilization of social science research and expertise in policy making is one of the recurring issues facing the social scientists not only in India but almost everywhere.

II

Much of what is said and written about utilization of social sciences is in fact a lament over their *non-utilization*. Many of the social scientists in academia complain of the non-utilization of their work and expertise. Similarly, those who are blamed for non-utilization, namely, the bureaucrats and policy makers, retort by hinting at the *non-utilizability* of social sciences. The form this dialogue takes is that of a confrontation and conflict where each of the two parties tries to play a superior role and decry the other.

When it is said that social sciences are not utilized, what does this mean? For one thing, it is specifically mentioned in regard to their non-utilization by the public authorities. And it may mean one or more of the following:

1. Researches done on the specific issue are not being consulted.
2. Suggestions offered by a given researcher have been ignored.
3. Social scientists are not involved in policy formulation.
4. Those social scientists who are involved are treated "shabbily" and their opinions do not prevail.
5. Only specialists from a single discipline (particularly from economics) are involved in policy making and planning, while other specialists are ignored.
6. The policy making and planning exercise suffers from a lack of social science orientation.

7. Social scientific researches relative to policy areas are not being conducted.
8. Qualified social scientists are not recruited to administration or are not given priority in recruitment.

Similarly, those who criticize social sciences as being "esoteric" and "non-utilizable" do so in one or more of the following senses:

1. Much of the social science research is *non-relevant* to policy issues.
2. Micro-level and descriptive research does not help much in taking decisions at the national level.
3. Social research at the macro level tends to be overly theoretical and "jargonized", and unnecessarily complicates simple issues.
4. Research findings do not exist on several issues of contemporary significance and policy decisions cannot wait for research to emerge with its findings after a considerable lapse of time.
5. All that the social scientists offer in committees and meetings as advice is not based on foundations of solid research. Personal, political, and ideological choices disguised as social science prescription cannot be accepted.
6. The social sciences are overselling their bill of goods. They do not have answers to all the problems, nor do they understand the constraints of the bureaucracy and of the political system in which policy makers and administrators have to function.

III

It must be admitted that there is a dynamic interrelationship between the three processes of creation, diffusion, and utilization. A narrower concept of "use" refers only to "application" of social science knowledge to any specific problem area. Introducing the idea of application to the sphere of creation of new knowledge leads to a distinction between "pure" and "applied" research (at times also called "action" research). However, a broader concept of use would refer to the utilization of knowledge also (1) for purposes of creating new knowledge (after all, it is on the foundation of existing knowledge of theory and methodology that new knowledge is created), and (2) for purposes of dissemination of social science culture; in addition, of course, it implies the application of social sciences to practical problems of society. A distinction should also be made between the "use" of a particular piece of research, and "use" of a "body of knowledge". In this sense, a deliberate rejection of a research would also qualify as an act of use. In other words, a conscious disregard of research involves an evaluative exercise and it should be differentiated from non-use because of ignorance on the part of the user. Further, non-use may also imply non-acceptance of the "interpretation" of the data or of "recommendations" made by the researcher. Any analysis of "use" therefore, must distinguish between use of theory, use of methodology, use of research findings, and use of interpretations. All the above relate to the broader distinction between the *use of social science knowledge* as against the *use of social scientists.*

It follows that the model of use should incorporate several categories of users rather than just one. Among the users of social science knowledge should be included fellow social scientists, colleagues from sister disciplines, students, administrators, planners and policy makers, and the wider public. Problems of utilization, non-utilization and underutilization of social science knowledge exist among all these members of the role-set of a social scientist and ought to be identified in order to draw an objective profile of utilization of social sciences in a given country. Based on the interrelationship between the type of knowledge and the type of users, the following matrix can be constructed:

Type of Users	Type of Knowledge					
	General orientation	*Theory*	*Methodology*	*Research findings*	*Interpretation of findings*	*Specific recommendation*
	1	*2*	*3*	*4*	*5*	*6*
1. Fellow colleagues	11	12	13	14	15	16
2. Colleagues from other disciplines	21	22	23	24	25	26
3. Students	31	32	33	34	35	36
4. Administrators, planners, policy makers	41	42	43	44	45	46
5. Public	51	52	53	54	55	56

It may be admitted that it is a simplified matrix; each of the boxes in this matrix can be further broken down into several sub-boxes. Problems of use, and of non-use, would then have to be located in each.

Broadly speaking, the users can be dichotomized as: (1) those within academia, and (2) those outside it. Even within academia, one finds a crisis of non-utilization, and this contributes to the relative neglect outside academia as well.

Within the academia, we may identify three categories of users, namely, fellow colleagues, colleagues from other disciplines, and students. One can also include a fourth category of academic administrators. The factors responsible for non-use of social sciences in this domain may now be noted as under:

Ambivalence Towards Interdisciplinarity

While considerable lip-service is paid to the new emphasis on interdisciplinary orientation, there is very little evidence of actual movement towards it. Increasing specializations even within one discipline are creating opportunities for separatism.

For example, the growing mathematization of economics has created barriers between the economists trained conventionally and those with a mathematical orientation. It is a commonplace complaint that many of the economists of the older generation, and several of the lecturers and students in affiliated colleges, find it difficult to read and understand journal articles in their own field because of the increasing use of mathematical language which they never learnt. There is also the complaint that economists who continue to be the favourites of government planning agencies perpetuated a philosophy of "economism" and systematically excluded other social sciences.

It is only in a few institutions of higher learning that students of a given discipline are given an exposure to several disciplines as part of their academic preparation. When research teams are constituted with people drawn from different disciplines they tend to be *multidisciplinary* rather than *interdisciplinary*. In such situations, the discipline of the team leader plays the dominant role, and other disciplines are allowed a limited play. Real integration of various orientations is rarely attempted. Now that the failures of a purely economic approach are being highlighted, one is puzzled by attempts more in the spirit of a "take-over" than of a "get-together". Disciplines compete rather than cooperate; they attempt to prove their superiority or distinctiveness, and they jealously guard their boundaries. The best example of such a futile battle can be seen in the relationship between the twin disciplines of sociology and social anthropology which have so much in common. For policy purposes a holistic and interdisciplinary perspective is needed which quarrelling social science disciplines fail to provide, and thus their immense policy potential remains underutilized.

It is not my intention to suggest that skills in individual disciplines are not needed. What I wish to emphasize is the need for training cadres of people who could be transdisciplinary in their orientation. Such people are needed in administration and in policy making fora, whom the culture of narrow academic specialization has failed to produce.

Ambivalence Towards Indigenous Scholarship

There is much truth in the allegation that many have not been able to decolonize their minds. There is so much fascination with the "foreign", verging almost on uncritical reverence, that we tend to neglect contributions by those from the "periphery".

This has several implications. Much foreign work may not be of immediate relevance to the practical concerns of a given society. What is generally sought in foreign writings is *theory*, which may still be parochial despite its claim to universality and therefore may not be applicable. Research done abroad may provide good insights and also methodological guidelines but the "findings" of such research are not utilizable; even research done by outsiders in a given country incorporates the biases of this outsider. The value of exposure to such material is not denied, but the relevance of it for policy purposes ought always to be questioned. Much more serious is the problem of neglect of work done by colleagues, or so-called "insiders", largely in the form of research in the local or national setting. A review of publications suggests that there is a greater tendency to quote and refer to foreign scholars than to local ones. Those indigenous scholars who are quoted, more often than not, are the "stars" of the profession, occupying positions of power. But seldom does a senior scholar allude to the work of a junior one. Thus, much local work done on problems of contemporary significance remains unnoticed because of the preference for alien scholarship, and neglect of work by compatriots. If even colleagues do not make use of local research, one can well understand its neglect by policy makers.

Information Gap

The remarks above relate to published research. An even more serious problem is that of publishing research findings. There is usually a lag of three to five years between the completion of research and the publication of the report, not to mention research which never reaches publication. Thus, by the time a book is published much data has become out-of-date and therefore remains only of academic interest. With the increasing cost of printing, books are generally priced prohibitively, making their purchase almost impossible not only for an individual scholar but also makes them inaccessible to the administrators, and to the common man; only interested students consult them in the libraries. Associated with high cost is the fact that in India most books are in English, competence in which is increasingly declining.

Another dimension of the information gap is the time lag between the publication of a book and its inclusion in a syllabus. To be sure, because of the bias against indigenous scholarship, very few books and research writings by local scholars are ever set in the curricula, and even those which receive such recognition may not necessarily be promoted by the teaching faculty. The procedure of curriculum framing is so tedious and tardy that it stifles all initiative. It may be noted that changes introduced in courses today become operative only after two years, thus a research report may reach the classroom only after seven to eight years of its completion.

We may now turn to the factors that account for the relative non-use or under-use of social sciences by those in the policy circles.

Supply-demand Mismatch

Users are constantly looking for material that is relevant to their concerns and readily available. Since not all research is carried out in response to policy needs, it does not get immediately utilized. The existing repertoire of research does not offer all the needed data. Social scientists, no doubt, possess the skills to handle a question the policy maker, or administrator might pose; but they take time to provide the answer. Immediately they can at best, suggest a framework, a perspective, to understand the problem; they can set out parameters and throw up possible hypotheses based on theory, or on previous research, and on their personal experience as participant observers. But concrete solutions to specific problems cannot be provided offhand. On the other hand, administrations are often confronted with the need for immediate action; they cannot wait until a research study is produced. Moreover, the larger the scale of the study, the greater the costs both in terms of time and money. This the administrator obviously cannot afford. He has to provide immediate interim measures based on whatever information he has, and to the best of his judgment. When social scientists are approached for advice, most often they are caught unprepared. If they venture to respond they end up giving their own impressions; and if they hesitate they are likely to be misunderstood as incompetent. With the growing demand for social science, the seniors of the profession are increasingly becoming involved in advisory committees and are thus left with little time to do research, or even to keep track of what is being written. A strange situation thus prevails where those who are not researching are performing an advisory role, and those who are researching are generally not consulted. There is a big problem of coping with the burgeoning demands, and of lack of communication between social science researchers and social science advisers. Users of social science research derive their opinions about the social sciences from their evaluation of the role of social science advisers.

Inadequacies of Social Science Research

Whether one calls it an inadequacy or not, it is certainly a limitation of social science research that it is a time-consuming activity. It does not produce instant results. Moreover, much of the work by individual researchers is in the nature of micro studies: small samples, selected areas, single communities, chosen variables. Such studies tend to dig deeper, not wider. The decision makers and policy framers operating at the macro level find it difficult to utilize micro studies to their advantage as they rightly question the degree of their generalizability. Social sciences in India do provide examples of some macro level studies, but these are either based on secondary data analysis, or are quasi-theoretical in nature. Efforts to synthesize several micro studies to draw up macro profiles are still inchoate. It must be acknowledged too that the strength of some of the social sciences—particularly sociology and social anthropology—lies in their capacity to operate at the micro level and to unravel many of the crucial processes at that level; to an administrator and planner, however, this appears to be too puny and minuscule to be useful. When he wants to plan, for example, something for rural India, he does not want a sociologist to inform him only about the particular village he has studied but about village India as a whole. Until we go "beyond the village" and talk about villages in the plural, we will not be able to establish rapport with policy framers.

Yielding to the temptation of relevant research, and the availability of funds for it, many social scientists also engage in "action research". But the validity of their findings is quite often questioned. It must be admitted that in our zest for jumping into the bandwagon some of us produce tons of trash and trivia, whereas the user is looking only for a pound of profundity.

Another inadequacy of social science research is its bias towards unidisciplinarity. Studies of the same phenomenon carried out by different specialists focus on certain aspects of it, with almost one-sided accentuation. Already there is criticism of the firm entrenchment of economists in government planning, but the answer to this lies neither in their dethronement, nor in the enthronement of any other social science discipline. Mere clamour for recognition, or a diatribe against another discipline, is obviously a poor way to prove competence and relevance. It would be wrong to say that economics is not needed just because sociology is also in demand. What needs to be emphasized is the point that a "single discipline rarely has an unassailable claim to solve a practical problem" because "policy problems rarely correspond in any *a priori* way with the conceptual structure of a single discipline" (OECD, 1977: 21).

The language used in the social sciences is often regarded as a barrier to communication. While a special dispensation is granted to an engineer or a natural scientist, it is generally believed that social phenomena should be comprehensible even to the non-specialist. The use of special concepts in social science writing is decried as jargon, and difficulty in the comprehension of a technical social science piece ensures its disregard and rejection. What the user needs is a readable document of reasonable proportions, not a mastodon couched in unintelligible jargon.

Lack of Consensus on Orientation

Various schools of thought exist in the social sciences, each contending for a place of prime and at times denigrating others. If conflicting perspectives are presented to the user, and he makes his own choice from among the alternatives, he will be charged guilty of rejecting several in favour of one and will allow the adherents of the former to complain of non-utilization. Further, unlike in the natural sciences, orientations in social sciences are often value-laden and ideological in character. It is also not uncommon for social scientists to subscribe to a political point of view, or an ideological stance; things said and written from such a perspective quite logically lead to debate and confrontation, and blur the distinction between politics and social science. Much of the concern shown for "commitment" is to be seen in this light. Lack of consensus among social scientists may help generate an intellectual debate—and in that sense serves a useful function for society—but it does not make social sciences any more amenable for policy use.

Conflict of Bureaucratic and Academic Cultures

In dealing with the problem of interaction between bureaucrats and academics, or policy makers and scholars, it must be realized that we are essentially dealing with a pattern of interaction between two subcultures each having its own conservative and progressive forces—the conservative forces trying to keep them insulated while progressive forces attempting to open apertures. The academic is torn between two loyalties—to his profession and to his country, so also is the bureaucrat. In order to maintain his professional prestige, the academic writes for a professional audience and thus becomes insulated; the professional bureaucrat also does not want to give up his prerogative of taking decisions, and acting on his own initiative rather than favouring external consultations. To quote Foster: "Bureaucrats, like all other human beings, jealously guard their traditional perquisites and positions, willingly surrendering vested interests only in exchange for something good or better. Consequently, rearrangements in role relations, which favour some and threaten others, always meet with resistance. In bureaucracies, this leads to organizational inflexibility..." (1973: 178). Bureaucratic response to academic "intrusion" is thus three-fold: (1) they are also competent in social sciences—have earned degrees in them, been trained in these disciplines when they joined the services, and are engaged in continuous fieldwork; (2) the social scientists do not know the structure and dynamics of administration and thus offer unrealistic and non-realizable solutions; and (3) they write for themselves and try to overawe bureaucrats with the monster of methodology or the dead weight of theory.

Policy as Politics

Policy making is a political act. Even when a bureaucrat is assigned the policy making responsibility he has an unwritten obligation to keep his political masters in good humour. The party in power is guided by the ideology or philosophy it subscribes to, on the basis of which it receives support from the electorate. It has to weigh the consequences of a policy decision in terms of its own stability. Such a bias does not permit selection of the best possible alternative. When policy makers seek assistance from the social scientist they want either a prescription for a workable strategy, a justification for their act in academic terms, or participation of the academics in the attainment of their goals. Those who provide this are regarded by them as "committed", and by others as "establishment-oriented". To an extent their social science expertise is utilized in the spirit in which it is made available—their advice is open to acceptance or rejection. Social scientists belonging ideologically to the opposite camp understandably complain of neglect. Seen objectively, both groups are ideologically committed and their claims and complaints must be seen from this angle. In a sense, criticism offered by opponents is utilized in that care is taken to reply to it or to improve the working of the system, or just to ignore it. Non-attached intellectuals—a category that can logically be conceived—are blissfully outside the power game, and if their formulations do not take into consideration this aspect of policy making, they are bound to be viewed as impractical. Much of the failure of economic planning is attributed to ignoring socio-cultural variables. The phrase "other things remaining equal" may be a laudable scientific caution but in the sphere of action these "other things" are quite important and they do not always remain equal.

IV

So far we have tried to analyze the factors that impede interplay between producers and users of knowledge. We may now briefly turn to the other dimension of the proposed matrix, namely, the typology of knowledge and the conception of use. While thinking about transfer of knowledge—that is dissemination (diffusion) of knowledge—one can identify six aspects of it: general orientation, specific theories, methodology of research, research findings, interpretation of findings, and specific recommendations for action. It is clear that different types of users will lay different emphases on these various components. For example, users within academia will regard theoretical and methodological aspects to be a priority concern, while users in administration and policy domain may have a disdain for theory and show greater concern for findings that are relevant to action.

It may be emphasized that the model employed here for studying the problem of use makes only an analytical distinction between users and producers of knowledge. Implicit is the suggestion that producer-user can be complementary roles of the same individual. One cannot be a good producer if one does not make use of available knowledge. Moreover, even use can produce knowledge. There is no one way traffic from knowledge to action. For action, further, not only social science knowledge is needed; knowledge from other sources is equally important and is, in fact, utilized. Even from within the social sciences, different types of knowledge may be needed at different stages of action. Just exactly how this happens, varies from situation to situation, and from problem to problem. Empirical evidence generated from different perspectives may present a decision maker with a real panorama to develop a proper fit, to work out a net balance of consequences, and to evaluate the costs involved in each of the possible alternatives. Thus, knowledge received from various sources goes through a process of, what may be called, *sanitization*, and the manner in which it gets reflected in policy, or in an implementation strategy, may be the result of this sanitizing and recombining exercise.

What goes into policy making is a whole chunk of knowledge derived through various channels, and not just research from a single source. This implies that the decision maker is not the sole user of social science knowledge; in a democratic process of decision making several actors make use of this knowledge and articulate their reactions. Such a feedback is equally a component of knowledge which the decision maker can ignore only at his peril.

This calls, therefore, for a broader interpretation of utilization. The extent to which social sciences are utilized depends upon their stage of development in terms of theory and methodology, and their state in a given country. There may be certain questions that existing social sciences may not be in a position to answer; there may be certain other questions which can be answered by the present state of knowledge but a country may lack the needed manpower or the skills to answer them. It could be claimed for example that social sciences in India have acquired considerable sophistication in the investigation and description of objective social reality but are still behind in theory. They do not yet possess adequate powers of prediction and prescription.

Social scientists can definitely make a contribution towards (1) the clarification of issues and provision of conceptual frameworks; (2) the assessment of different assumptions and estimation of likely costs of alternative strategies; and (3) narrowing down the sphere of uncertainties. It is doubtful however whether they can suggest definitively any *oughts* and *musts* in the policy domain (if so they act not as social scientists but in their other roles). They can certainly assist in developing strategies for a chosen policy option or a stated goal. They can carry out evaluative studies to assess the effectiveness of a programme or the consequences—both intended and unintended—that any given programme may have.

The broader role of social sciences should however not be underestimated. They constitute an important part of the academic culture. And since socialization in this culture through the process of formal education is becoming universal the social science sub-culture is increasingly being internalized. Today social sciences in India are a sizeable enterprise. All the universities and a myriad colleges teach courses in them. Those who enter administration or even politics are likely to be graduates in arts and social sciences. They thus carry with them in their new roles the elements of this culture. Their thinking and their actions are thus influenced by this exposure. Moreover training in the social sciences—particularly their applied aspects—is also imparted to civil servants when they are inducted into the service.

The amount of research conducted and published in social sciences also gives one an indication of the importance assigned to it and of the increasing user clientele. The number of research departments within the government and even government funding available for research through agencies such as the Indian Council of Social Science Research and the University Grants Commission is yet another indicator of the growing recognition. The introduction of teaching in social sciences to the graduating students in such fields as agriculture engineering and medicine is also an example of the acknowledgement of their utility in professional education. One may go a step further and say that while social sciences have been derided for their jargon, their vocabulary is becoming a part of common parlance in administrative and elite circles—a good example of the diffusion of social science culture, and hence of utilization of social science knowledge.

It is equally important to acknowledge that it is not only social science knowledge which is being used, but that social scientists are increasingly involved, drawn from different disciplines. Social scientists in the universities and research institutions receive support for research from the government, which continues to be the major fund giver; these funds are not only for research in the priority areas defined by the government but also for research in areas of interest to individual researchers. This has generated a climate of research in the country, and also promoted a debate regarding the use and relevance of research which, to me, appears to be a healthy trend.

Doubts are quite often raised about funded research being influenced by the funding agency. The word "influence" in this context connotes several meanings: that the integrity of the scholar is questionable, that the research will be biased in favour of the status quo, that the topic for research is not of academic relevance, that the research will merely be of the fact-finding type, that the "findings" and "recommendations" will be dictated by the fund giver. While there is some substance in all these allegations and they may apply to certain types of research, a few researchers, and some of the funding agencies, they cannot be generalized. For one thing, it must be realized that in a country like India where the government is the principal source of funding for all academic work, reliance must be placed on this funding source if money is needed to carry out research or even eke out a living as an academic. Secondly, it would be hypocritical to assert that a scholar opposed to the prevailing ideology has a right to choose his own research theme but to deny the same right to the scholar who subscribes to the policy and goals of the government of the day. Thirdly, it is agreed that the availability of funds for research in a priority area may influence selection of a research topic (which can also be academically important and challenging) but such selection does not prevent the researcher from studying it scientifically. Fourthly, one may question the interpretation of the data but not the empirical evidence if it has been collected properly. In this connection, let me quote the findings of research carried out by Jim Thomas (1982) on "The Impact of Government Sponsorship in Social Science". He compared the funded and non-funded research on police (for the period 1960-1977) in terms of paradigm, data manipulation, theoretical perspective, and problematic. The study was "an attempt to examine the contention of some critics of federal sponsorship of social research that sponsors and their recipients may control, or at least disproportionately influence, the production of knowledge". A content analysis of five major journals does not support the contention. The data would, in fact, appear to challenge the assertions... in that no evidence was found to support the hypotheses that funded research:

1. encourages recipients to adopt a positivist research perspective to a greater degree than non-funded research;
2. influences recipients to choose narrowly defined research areas dictated by policy needs of agencies;
3. leads to an increasing use of statistical data manipulation;
4. threatens the independence of social research at the technical level because of acceptance of "official" categories, methods, or agency views;
5. is "control-oriented" or addresses means for directly resolving social, political or economic conflicts; and
6. is necessarily more politically conservative in that it supports the social or political status quo more strongly than does non-funded research (Thomas, 1982:360).

To make the point clear, let me state the position once again:

1. Not all funded research is geared to policy concerns; similarly, there can be research on policy issues which may be undertaken without any funding support.
2. Funding need not necessarily influence the findings; it can, however, promote research on topics that are of concern to the funding agency. These topics can be viewed as relevant irrespective of funding considerations.
3. The research interests of a scholar may coincide with the relevance criteria of the fund-giver and therefore the former may approach the latter for support.

4. Commitment is a loosely defined word and is quite often used in a pejorative sense. Those who advocate commitment take the view that social sciences are not value free. Since conflicting ideologies may prevail, one cannot expect consensus on commitment to any; different people may be committed to different ideologies. To be conservative is one sort of commitment; to be opposed to it is another type of commitment. If commitment is regarded as desirable, both types of commitment have to be acknowledged. There should also be a place for the kind of scholarship which distinguishes between political and ideological commitment and commitment to the canons of science. The notion that only committed social scientists contribute to policy requires serious scrutiny.

I hope that the paper did not give the impression of being written by the pen of the complacent. It is not the intention to suggest that all is well with the social sciences and that there is no crisis of their non-utilization. It is argued that the problem of non-utilization exists not only vis-à-vis the people outside the academia, that there is also a need to put our own house in order and to be clear about what we can offer at the present stage of our knowledge to those who seek our advice. To know our limitations is as important as knowing our strengths.

Social sciences have reached the stage where their general validity and relevance to policy matters particularly in the area of development is recognized. Probably, there is more demand than can be met either in terms of social science knowledge, or by the available social science manpower. There are many questions for which we do not have any answer, nor even the data; and there is a need for a sort of prospective planning to anticipate future demands likely to be made on social sciences and to prepare to meet them rather than waiting for an agency to commission work. If knowledge is to remain ahead of action, the producer of knowledge must attend to this responsibility rather than be satisfied with the existing intellectual kit. Social sciences do sell but we must continue enhancing their marketability. By better performance within the academic system one can ensure better and greater utilization. One would then attract the clientele, rather than running after it.

This is, of course, not to deny the need for strengthening communication and dialogue between the government and social scientists, and promoting the interest of bureaucrats and policy makers in social science knowledge which would help bridge the credibility and perception gap, enrich the knowledge base, and widen the scope of its use.

The OECD report on *Utilization of the Social Sciences in Policy Making* rightly asserts: "The social sciences cannot be considered simply as instruments for administrative management; nor is their policy relevance confined to some residual area of concerns labelled 'social policy'. The social impact of social sciences is, therefore, not limited to their direct utilization by public authorities. In their attempt to describe and analyze social reality more effectively, they provide the individual with deeper insights into his community and, conversely, contribute to mould the ways in which the community sees itself" (Ibid.:13). The social sciences thus perform not only a manipulative role (as is implicit in the concept of use in the natural sciences) but more importantly a role to enhance our capabilities to comprehend, to enlarge our cognitive horizons, and expose us to a range of alternatives from which to choose.

Social sciences are needed for purposes of policy development, and policy is needed for the development of social sciences. Action on both fronts must go hand in hand.

References

Atal, Yogesh, 1976, *Social Sciences: The Indian Scene,* Abhinav Publications, New Delhi.

Clammer, John, 1982, Soci*ology and Development: Problems and Prospects from the Perspective of South and Southeast Asia,* Regional Institute of Higher Education for Development, Singapore.

Dube, S.C. (ed.), 1976, *Social Sciences and Social Relations: Role of Social Sciences in Contemporary India,* Indian Institute of Advanced Study, Simla.

Foster, George M., 1973, *Traditional Societies and Technological Change* (second edition), Allied Publishers, Bombay.

Lindblum, Charles A. Cohen, and David K. 1979, *Usable Knowledge: Social Science and Social Problem Solving,* Yale University Press, New Haven.

OECD, 1977, *The Utilization of the Social Sciences in Policy Making,* Organization for Economic Cooperation and Development, Paris.

Ratnam, K.J. (ed.), 1980, *Social Sciences: In Response to Policy Needs,* UNESCO office of the Regional Adviser for Social Sciences in Asia and the Pacific, Bangkok.

Rein, Martin, 1980, "Methodology for the Study of the Interplay between Social Science and Social Policy" in *International Social Science Journal, Vol.* XXXII, No. 2, pp. 361-368.

Thomas, Jim, 1982, "Federal Funding and Policing Research" *Knowledge: Creation, Diffusion, Utilization*, Vol. 3, No. 3, pp. 339-369.

Weiss, Caroul H. (ed.), 1977, *Using Social Research in Public Policy Making,* Lexington Books, Lexington, Mass.

8

The Studies of the Village in India*

I

Pursuit of knowledge is guided by the inner dynamics of a discipline as well as by the operating culture of the surrounding social milieu. While theoretical development and methodological sophistication set limits to a scientific quest, the choice of the research themes from among the available alternatives is largely governed by extra-academic considerations—concerns of the state, one's ideological predilections, influence of the peer group, and the like. A socially relevant problem may become a sociologically significant research question, provided the researcher observes the rules of the game; a novice or an ideologue, on the other hand, may make social science a handmaiden of the values to which he is "committed". Outcome of the exercise apart, intellectual styles exhibit a pattern of fads and fashions; some topics become fashionable and then suddenly fade out and are replaced by new fashions. In some cases, the trends set may lead to the creation of new branches and specialisms, and thus contribute to the growth of the discipline, provide description of the social reality in a scientific manner, arrive at fruitful hypotheses, improve theoretical formulations, and refine tools of research.

---

* Reprinted from Yogesh Atal, *Social Sciences: The Indian Scene*, Abhinav Publications, New Delhi, 1976 as Chapter 9.

A phase came in Indian sociology and anthropology when there was heavy accent on village studies; over a period of time, it gave way to studies of change—particularly, directed culture change. The trend finally culminated into the more general theme of modernization; currently, Indian sociologists are engaged in the exploration of the several facets of the overpowering process of modernization—urbanization, educational expansion, political mobilization, breakdown of tradition, and economic development.

The history of the studies of village community in India may be regarded as young as the Indian independence. No doubt, there were, in the past, some sporadic attempts by British scholars and administrators to investigate the aspects of rural life, but they did not generate a "movement" in the academia. In the early years of independence, the twin disciplines of sociology and social anthropology directed their attention towards the village, and a number of significant contributions were made. Almost all researchers in these two disciplines—senior scholars, scholars working for their Ph.D. and the M.A. students writing their dissertations based on field work engaged themselves in the study of the village community in India. The village, in fact, became the meeting ground for the practitioners of the two disciplines who were earlier engaged in two different styles of enquiry; the sociologist was much nearer to the Indologist, and to the armchair analyst of secondary data; the anthropologist has his concern with the primitive and the past, and endeavoured to be the know-all of the various branches of the overarching science of Man.

The discontinuity in the established tradition came when the anthropologist entered the non-tribal village under the pressures of a changing theory and in response to the challenge that the new adventure offered. This somehow coincided with the new government's commitment to the revitalization of the rural sector with an accent on the improvement of agriculture and related activities. This occasioned the sociologist to complain that his terrain has been intruded by the anthropologist who has no office in the village and whose methods of work, suitable for the tribal study, are inappropriate and inadequate for the investigation of the rural phenomena. But the anthropologist could not be dislodged, and the sociologist also arrived on the scene with almost the same kit-bag; both explored the village with a continued reciprocal ambivalence. Thus, depending upon their academic degrees and designations, their contributions were classified under rural sociology or rural anthropology; contentwise, there was, however, little to justify such superficial distinction.

The manner in which rural studies developed in India is vastly different from the type of rural sociology practised in the West. In the United States, for example, there is a much longer tradition of rural research. Rural sociology began there as a response to the practical needs of the administration regarding the factual reports on the farm situation. The Country Life Commission, appointed in 1907 by President Roosevelt, pioneered rural studies and published several detailed reports. The first phase of their consolidation and systematization was also oriented to practical needs with very little concern for theory. Thus, J.M. Gillette's book, *Constructive Rural Sociology* (1913), was written with the following four objectives: (i) to take a full inventory of the conditions of life in rural communities; (ii) to discover their tendencies and deficiencies; (iii) to map out special problems; and (iv) to indicate ways of betterment according to the best ideals of social life. It is only in 1929, when Sorokin and Zimmerman published their work that theoretical foundations of rural sociology were laid in the United States.

In the courses on rural sociology taught in India, prior to the village studies movement, there was an unimaginative copying of the West; text books analyzing American rural scene were used with a total neglect of the village in India. This is, of course, understandable in view of the fact that no worthwhile studies of the village life in India were then available, barring official statistics at the macro-level. The realization came rather late that the United States has a farm population but there are no villages, and that this non-urban population is a very small proportion of the country's total population. Therefore, categories of analysis used in the study of American farm life, as well as the findings of such studies, had little, if any, relevance to the Indian rural scene. But the university professoriate in India continued the use of this material in the courses; even now some centers adhere to this tradition.

The real breakthrough came when the anthropologists got interested in the study of the peasantry. It was a matter of historical accident that the discipline of anthropology, despite its etymology and stated definition of scope, became synonymous with tribal studies. The "other cultures" that the anthropologist studied were those of the primitives living in relative isolation, cut off not only from the civilized world but also from their own past, in the absence of a written language. Such a narrower definition of the discipline was not acceptable to some scholars, who broadened its scope to include, on the one hand, analyses of ancient India, classical Greece and Rome, Egypt and China, and, on the other peasant societies and complex civilizations of the contemporary era. It was shift in attention to which Robert Redfield gave his seal of approval: "...anthropologists have moved very rapidly to accept a part of the responsibility for studying civilized people, nation-states, and such worldwide events as industrialization and urbanization... Today anthropology...studies just about everything human" (Redfield, 1956:9-10). Noting a similar trend in India, S.C. Dube remarked in his Presidential Address to the social anthropology section of the Third All India Sociological Conference in 1958: "Anthropologists are no longer concerned primarily, or even mainly, with the study of tribal cultures; in increasing numbers they are now operating nearer home in village communities where they have discovered challenging possibilities of theoretical and applied social science research."

The difficulties encountered in the investigation of the tribal communities, using the holistic and microcosmic frame of reference, initiated a process of re-examination of the anthropological approach. The worldwide phenomenon of culture-contact enveloped the tribal people and gave rise to a series of transformations in the culture and social structure of the societies of the so-called primitive world. To their dismay, anthropologists found that none of the living societies is nearer the ideal of a "folk society". In its place, they discovered a sort of folk-urban continuum along which the various societies could be placed. The transformation of the "folk" into "peasant" community was distinctly noticeable. Thus, along with the subject matter of his study, the anthropologist also moved and began studying peasant society and culture. In doing so, while he introduced some newer categories of analysis, he retained the time-honoured technique of participant observation and treated the village as an "isolable" unit, rather than an "isolate". It was realized that the "whole" of the village community was not complete, that it was a part of the wider whole, of greater society.

Theoretically oriented authors provided a framework for the analysis of such little communities. The newer concepts of indigenous civilization, great and little tradition, spread, and networks were evolved and utilized by the researchers in the new setting. In brief, following factors may be listed which have facilitated inclusion of village studies in the discipline of anthropology:

1. Attempts to broaden the definition of anthropology as a science of Man at all levels of cultural development.
2. Recognition of the fact that simple, isolated tribal folks are only an ideal construct and that culture-contact has already broken their isolation. In fact, some allege that these were wrongly treated as isolated groups.

3. Realization of the fact that the majority of the world population is rural and it cannot be neglected by a student of society.
4. Attraction towards the new field of study full of research possibilities.
5. Better facilities for work in villages compared to the tribal settlement; the villages are proximate, they are easily accessible, and they pose little language problem for the local (native) researchers.
6. Applicability of the traditional anthropological techniques of research in the study of the village communities.
7. Need for the study of the village communities in view of the several forces of change being introduced from outside. It was realized that if these communities were not studied now, the currently existing patterns will remain unreported as they might disappear or get modified under the impact of induced change.

Following the general trend, Indian anthropology also moved in the direction of rural studies, courageously breaking the tradition of tribal ethnographies. Both foreign and Indian scholars chose to explore the village in India.

There were, however, some additional factors, which promoted interest in village studies in India.

Though the anthropologists working among Indian tribes were familiar with the fact of culture contact and change, they largely followed the tradition of ethnography and wrote monographs in the idiom of an eternal ethnographic present. They devoted very little space to the processes of culture change, and whenever they did, they focussed more on the problems created by the haphazard and unhealthy contacts with the outside world. Their well-intended concern for gradual extinction of tribal culture was grossly misunderstood and they were accused of being supporters of the idea of an anthropological zoo. Notwithstanding the emphasis on the linkage between tribal religion and Hinduism in the writings of scholars like Hutton, anthropology suffered from the stigma of being a *colonial* discipline interested in the preservation of the exotic and the queer. In response to such a volley of hostile criticism, conscientious anthropologists felt the need of demonstrating that their science was not oriented toward the status quo; that they were interested both in the static as well as dynamic aspects of the society. As a result, several studies on cultural change were undertaken. This necessitated a change in the perspective and broadening of the horizons. Tribals living in rural settlements and even in industrial settings were studied and their relationships with the non-tribal population were mapped.

At this critical phase, Indian anthropologists were helped by the developments in theory and in the methodology of anthropological research. Of particular importance were the writings of Robert Redfield. Some of the students inspired by his conceptual framework came to India with a view to testing its applicability and enriching it with empirical evidence. Indian scholars followed suit.

It must be said that in the latter half of the 1950s American rural sociologists also began evincing interest in the rural studies in India. As is well known, though rural sociology continued to grow in the USA, its farm population continued its declining trend—from 29.9 per cent in 1920 to 15.3 per cent in 1950 to about 13 per cent in 1960. This was probably one of the reasons that the American rural sociologist shifted his focus from broad-based studies to intensive type, and changed his single cultural orientation to a cross-cultural one. The first resulted in acceptance of the approach of micro-research, and the second brought him out to other countries breaking his geographic isolation and affecting prevalent parochialism. There was also a practical responsibility on his shoulders. The US government, giving assistance to underdeveloped agricultural countries under the aid programme, was interested in both gaining knowledge about the social life of these countries, and in providing technical personnel to offer expert advice on developmental problems. Through several funding agencies, India obtained the services of the rural sociologists and anthropologists. A number of research teams arrived under different auspices to study various aspects of village life.

It must, however, be reminded that interest in rural life is not altogether new. Even the British administrators and scholars wrote about the system of land tenure, customary law and the functioning of village councils. The District Gazetteers, tribes and castes compilations, and the writings of Baden-Powell, Henry Maine, Charles Metcalfe, Darling, and Ibbetson are representative of this trend. Finding considerable contrast with the social situation obtaining in the West, these scholars treated the villages as being static, as practitioners of a sort of primitive communism, and functioning as "little republics". Later, a series of socio-economic surveys of the villages were conducted by the government.[1] It was this material about the life led "behind the mudwalls" that formed the base for the fresh series of sociologically oriented empirical studies on the village. These studies sought to describe the village life in different parts of the country with a view to examining the validity of the generalizations made by earlier scholars and to understanding prevailing social structure. The idea of rural welfare inspired by Mahatma Gandhi and Rabindranath Tagore also gave impetus to village studies.

Gandhi felt strongly that real India lives in the villages and it is there that the torch of freedom is to be lit. He hinted at several problems that warranted attention and systematic investigation—caste prejudices, untouchability, rural poverty and indebtedness, feudal exploitation, and general backwardness of the economy. Independent India accepted the teachings of Mahatma Gandhi and gave a concrete shape to his concern with the village life. With the Five-Year Plans, the Government inaugurated a new phase of economic development and social reconstruction. Rural upliftment became her major goal, which was tried to be achieved through a process of directed culture change under the auspices of the Community Development Programme launched in October 1952. In this massive exercise, the social scientist was called upon to help in the areas of human relations, social structure, and culture. This came as a challenge in two ways: (a) he was to provide the needed information to the development personnel; whatever information was available was grossly inadequate and therefore research was needed to generate relevant information; (b) even academically, it became imperative to document the existing social structure as it was being exposed to the throes of change. The sociologist-anthropologist participated in several ways in the rural community development programme. He provided detailed full-length monographic studies of the villages from different parts of India; he associated with the programme as consultant, adviser, incharge of action programme, and as a trainer; he conducted specific benchmark surveys and pilot studies; he carried out analytical studies of culture change; he prepared detailed case studies of particular action programmes; and he did some evaluation work.

Rural studies thus gained a momentum after independence. Specializations were introduced in this field in different social sciences. They also paved the way for the entry of social sciences in institutions teaching agricultural sciences, and in the newly established rural institutes, as well as in the training and orientation centres set up by the Department of Community Development.

II

It is said that it is not only the discipline of sociology, which is new in the old society of India, even the sociological profile of this society is still in the mill. Doubtless, there are scores of writings on India, which have fascinated Western scholarship, and on which have capitalized the Indian pundits. But these writings have done much to distort the Indian reality, and have hampered the growth of realistic sociology, which would replace ritualistic Indology. Srinivas decried this tendency while explicating the significance of village studies; he wrote:

> There is among our educated people, an unstated but nonetheless real and deep-seated assumption that what is written is true, and the older a manuscript, the more true its contents.
>
> Learning is almost synonymous with pouring over palm leaf .... Indology has come to be regarded as knowledge about India's past. Any suggestion that Indology should include the study of tribes and villages which are in existence today would be regarded as too absurd to merit consideration. Caste in Vedas and in Manu ought to be studied but caste as a powerful force in modern Indian life ought not to be (see Srinivas in Desai, 1969:735).

The profile of India provided by the indological writings was aptly termed by Srinivas as "book-view" and "upper caste-view".

So decisive was the influence of these "historical" writings that several of the sociologists in India, in their enthusiasm for a special "Indian sociology", engaged in the wholesale trans-shipment of Indology without even bothering to recast it in a sociological frame. The glare of the ancient was so blinding that Indian social system was equated with Hindu social system, and Manu's prescriptions were taken as descriptions of a living social reality. The important distinction between the *was*, the *ought*, and the *is* was conveniently ignored. Several informed commentaries on ancient texts did, however, appear from the pen of sociologists who valued library research, and who preferred to operate at an "all-India" level. Although the sociological relevance of such literature is undeniable, they cannot be regarded as sociology per se.

Economists also handled the rural sector but largely at the macro-level, and mostly through secondary data. There were, however, some attempts by economists, and social workers, to study the village life from the point of view of economics, and material well-being: conditions of life, income, land tenure, rural economic problems and the like. As Mukherjee rightly pointed out:

> the emphasis was laid...on purely economic categorization of rural society, and even the *social relations* which the villagers had evolved with reference to their economic organization were not attended to properly or at all [see in Desai, 1969:809].

Mukherjee further comments:

> Indeed, we know very little today about the structural and functional alignments in village society consequent to the economic activities of the people, not to speak of other aspects of their life. For, the preoccupation of the social scientists with the economics of rural society which became more and more pronounced since 1940s began to push the living persons in the background; and instead of presenting the villagers as *social beings* presented them...as abstract economic and social categories [Ibid.: 810].

Thus, both sociologists and economists, operating at the macro level, and content with library research of the armchair variety left the living reality almost untouched. In such a milieu, the initiation of empirical research—survey type as well as ethnographic-monographic (case study)—was a welcome trend and had almost a thrust of a movement in the 1950s in India. This trend was led by social-cultural anthropologists, both Indian and foreign. Among the Indian pioneers were Professors D.N. Majumdar, M.N. Srinivas and S.C. Dube. These leaders of the profession had a large following of rural researchers. It is significant that these scholars came out with three major publications on the village in India, all in the year 1955 and all summarizing the findings of field work carried out in the villages from different parts of India. Thus, Majumdar edited two volumes under the title *Rural Profiles;* Srinivas published an anthology on India's villages, compiling ethnographic accounts on individual villages earlier published in the then called *Economic Weekly.* Dube's *Indian Village* was the first full-length monograph on a Telengana village, Shamirpet.

In the same year, University of Chicago published another collection of essays edited by McKim Marriott under the title *Village India.* Several other articles, and M.A. and Ph.D. dissertations, on various aspects of village life were later published in the same decade. Mention may be made of *Caste and Communication in an Indian Village* (Majumdar, 1958), *The Twice Born* (Carstairs, 1957), *India's Changing Villages* (Dube, 1958), *Caste and the Economic Frontier* (Bailey, 1958), *After a Century and a Quarter* (Ghurye, 1960), *Village Life in Northern India* (Lewis, 1958), *Caste and Kinship in Central India* (Mayer, 1960), *Six Villages of Bengal: A Socio-Economic Survey* (Mukherjee, 1957) and *Behind Mudwalls* (Wiser and Wiser, 1951).

While these studies received widespread recognition, and found a place in the university curricula, the practitioners of anthropology who were engaged in rural research were the target of considerable criticism by physical anthropologists on the one hand, and sociologists on the other. In the gatherings of the former, they were considered as sociologist-converts because they were no longer studying tribal societies. Some sociologists, in turn, treated them as intruders rather than persons in the same boat. It sound strange that while the physical anthropologist in his quest for the "missing link" had turned a primatologist and had quite justifiably gone down to lemurs and langurs, he hated the legitimate ascendancy of the social anthropologist from the primitives to the peasantry and beyond. As a student of Social Man, the visit of the social anthropologist to a village cannot be regarded as intrusion or encroachment either. Sociologists treating him as an outsider, or a renegade, forget the crucial point that no theory of society can be built without examining the varied manifestations of human social behaviour in different kinds of societal arrangements. It seems paradoxical that while the non-village type sociologists found merit in free borrowing from Indological and even scriptural literature, they advocated refusal of visa to serious sociological work done by a fellow anthropologist.

R.N. Saksena has been quite vocal about this, though somewhat ambivalent. In his Presidential Address to the Fourth All India Sociological Conference, held in Calcutta in 1959, and in a number of articles which produced verbatim some of the paragraphs from the same address (including his note published in the *American Sociological Review* in 1962), he has commented upon the need to separate sociology from social anthropology, and even Indian sociology from Western sociology. Although he conceded the point that "the anthropologists and sociologists have repeatedly discovered each other in the same situation" and that "such an union proves to be extremely rewarding", he feels strongly that inclusion of social anthropology in the sociology courses "gives an indication of indefiniteness of the academic status acquired by sociology". For him, sociology is a "mother science to other social disciplines. But in India it is a case where the mother finds that the child has grown so big that it is difficult to hold". He is particularly critical of village studies which "reflect the microcosmic approach" because it has "some appeal to cultural anthropologist".[2] He regards the approach as inappropriate because "one cannot ignore the fundamental fact that the Indian village is a community". Many would find it difficult to appreciate this criticism of his. Microcosmic approach in anthropology was developed for the study of little communities; and if the Indian village is a community, such an approach should be regarded as ideal. Of course, if his worry is about the representative character of the study—that is generalizability of the findings at an all India level—then it is well-founded. Even students of village studies have acknowledged this fact. Dube, for example, has responded to this criticism thus: "What we lose by not working on an extensive and statistically adequate sample, we more than compensate by acquiring depth and coverage of overt and covert norms in our analysis... Anthropologists can remain unrepentant advocates of single village studies...for the village as a culture-bearing unit does mirror certain significant aspects of the region and the nation" (Dube, 1958a).

The rise of rural studies in India has generated a concern among scholars regarding a "sociology for India". While the propagators of village studies emphasized the need for hard facts, sociologists like Saksena argued, the "sociology in India cannot be entirely objective in its content and approach". He would like to lay greater stress on abstruse philosophy. A similar view is also expressed by Louis Dumont and David Pocock who, in their editorial to the inaugural number of *Contributions to Indian Sociology*, have recommended that "the first condition for a sound development of sociology of India is to be found in the establishment of proper relationship between it and classical Indology" (1957:7). They firmly believe that India should be treated as a unity and the studies should follow the pattern of a descriptive sociology. For them, descriptive sociology is a sociology of values. They would like to de-emphasise regional differences; "the nightmare of perpetual diversity" can be banished, they argue, if we accept the principle that "the constancy which we cannot find at the level of individual beings is very often revealed when we rise to the level of relations between these beings".

The strongest refutation to this position has come from F.G. Bailey. He argues that the approach of Indology is vastly different from that of sociology. The former emphasizes on the unique while the latter "wants to find out what India has in common with other societies... A definition of caste, which rules out comparison with, for instance, the southern states of America or even South Africa, is useless for comparative sociology. The unique is scientifically incomprehensible".

Relying only on values, or on social philosophy is to practise culturology and not sociology. A careful reading of the essay by Dumont and Pocock would, however, reveal that the position taken by them is somewhat exaggerated. They have certainly not decried fieldwork, as did Saksena. They have only started worrying about a frame in which the data could be fitted. Theirs is a plea for the systematization and synthesis of data with a view to presenting a sociological profile of India; this is different from the chauvinistic demand for the creation of a different sociology for India.

While the debate continues, a majority among the profession finds the demand for Indian sociology as paradoxical and unpragmatic. The distinction between sociology and social anthropology is also gradually eroding.

It need be stressed that even in the West, where such artificial distinction originated, there is considerable rethinking going on.

Thus Don Martindale remarks:

> ...Apart from differences, which emerge directly out of its peculiar historical context, it would be hard to say in what manner in the long run the theories of anthropology will differ from those of sociology [Martindale, 1960: 44].

Writing in the same vein, and commenting on the relationship between the two disciplines, particularly in the context of India, Bottomore has this to say:

> ...as the primitive societies regarded as the preserve of the social anthropologist have more or less disappeared so to some extent the special prerogatives of the sociologist in studying advances societies have been challenged. Among contemporary societies, there is a very important category of those, which are neither primitive nor industrially advanced. In such societies, of which India is an outstanding example, the distinction between sociology and social anthropology has little meaning. Sociological research in India, whether it is concerned with industrialization

> and its effects, is, and should be, carried out by sociologists and social anthropologists. There is a real opportunity in India for the traditional division between these disciplines to be overcome.... The development of social sciences in India and the diminishing dependence upon foreign educational resources will give an opportunity for a real integration of the methods and concepts of two disciplines in terms of the problems and research tasks relevant to Indian social life [Bottomore, 1962: 58].

A close association between sociology and social anthropology has also been very strongly recommended by the Review Committee on Sociology appointed by the Indian University Grants Commission in 1961. The report, published in 1966, disapproves of the tendency to treat these two as "completely different subjects", because "social anthropology is everywhere rapidly becoming a part of sociology" (pp. 26-27). The Committee recommended:

> that in universities which already have strong departments of sociology, social anthropology should be developed within their fold. On the other hand, in universities with sociologically oriented departments of social anthropology, it would be an advantage to initiate studies in sociology within their fold [p. 27].

III

Village studies movement in India has gone through a series of phases. As we noted, it began in the pre-independence period largely as a concern of the administrator, and was led by the practitioners of the discipline of economics; sociologists and social anthropologists arrived on the rural scene much later, and mostly after independence. They began their work in the style of an ethnographer, concentrating on a single village and following a holistic approach. It may be noted that the so-called microcosmic approach of the anthropologists, developed and practised by them in the tribal settings, treated tribe as a unit of study, which consisted of several villages; the villages were parts of the wider whole of the tribe. Application of the same approach in the rural areas was, however, different; in the latter case, the village was treated as a unit of study, a community social system, a "whole" of a sort. Thus, in a sense, anthropology in the rural setting adopted a still smaller unit for observation and reporting than in the case of tribal studies. The critics of anthropological studies of village have missed this crucial methodological point. They were arguing about the non-applicability of the method because it was meant for microcosms; the point that they miss, however, is that it is in the context of rural village that microcosmic approach has been applied in the true sense of the term. In the case of tribal ethnographies, the village does not figure so prominently as the stage of operations. Although "happenings" are observed in some villages, they are generalized for the tribe as a whole. In the case of rural studies, the village is both the unit of observation as well as of reporting; generalizations are made for the village "as a whole" and not beyond.

Quite expected, students of the village trained in the ethnographic tradition soon discovered that the village is not an isolate, although it is easily isolable. They exploded the myth of "little republics" and identified the factors that gave the village its unity, and the extensions, which linked it with wider and higher strata—territorial, relational, and religious. It is in this context that Robert Redfield's seminal concepts of indigenous civilization, little community, peasant society, and great and little tradition were examined, and their validity tested empirically. Taking clues from Redfield, and also from Srinivas, concepts of spread (local, regional, and all-india) and sanskritization (1952), McKim Marriott (1955) came up with two complementary concepts explicating the twin processes of universalization and parochialization. Oscar Lewis added to this inventory the concept of rural cosmopolitanism. A critical examination of these concepts led S.C. Dube (1958a) to propose a five-fold classification of Indian tradition; he tentatively listed them as classical, regional, local, western, and emergent national.

While researchers continued their village studies in the model of an ethnography, these concepts offered them with useful talking points. In the process, the style of description changed; analytical categories began to be used and methodological innovations were made.

Debate on concepts and methodology led to the diversification of village studies. Questions of representativeness promoted interest in comparative studies: more than one village, in the same or in a different culture area, was chosen for purposes of comparison. Rather than studying all aspects of life in a village, attention was concentrated in specific aspects—caste, family, group dynamics and factionalism, economic life and Jajmani system, village pantheon and the like. Efforts have also been made to study the same institution in a number of villages.

Introduction of the comparative approach necessitated proper and usable definition of the key concepts—village, caste, joint family. Of these three concepts, very little has been written on the concept of village; the definition given by the census has generally been accepted. There are instances where administrative definition was found unacceptable. Two illustrations will suffice: (1) in Rajasthan one of the places was, on popular demand, classified as town but later, upon the introduction of Panchayati Raj, political leadership of the community managed to reclaim its village status; (2) the satellite villages, called Nagla in Uttar Pradesh, are generally included as part of the core village though they possess, in many cases, all the sociological attributes of separate village community. Based on these considerations the present author ignored the revenue definition and treated a Nagla as a village in his study in *Local Communities and National Politics* (1971).

Attempts have also been made to classify the villages. Thus, some have taken the degree of nucleation as the key classificatory variable and talked about nucleated and dispersed villages. The concept of nucleated village includes the core village and the surrounding satellites. Similarly, coastal villages have been identified as a separate type. Studies have also been made of the fringe villages. In terms of social demography, classification based on the size of the settlement, and the number of ethnic groups (single caste versus multi-caste villages) is also in vogue. In terms of economic pursuit, while there is recognition of the presence of fishing and pastoral villages, studies have mostly concentrated on agricultural villages. A unique village from the Kulu valley has also been reported which has managed to keep itself more or less completely insulated from the rest of the village of the region by physically shutting its doors off to the outside world, by speaking its own language, and by practising its own culture (Rosser, 1955).

The most talked about concept in Indian rural sociology is that of caste. Whether the title of the study emphasizes village, or caste, it is the latter which invariably holds the floor. Village studies came in for heavy criticism because of this "obsession" with caste. The fact, however, remains that caste is a vital element of Indian society, and its neglect in study would have made the entire exercise worthless. It is only the students of village who started empirical investigation of this most complex phenomenon of Indian social structure. The great gap between the ideological precepts and the living reality—between the text and the present-day context—that they discovered was an eye-opener. While the urban-based armchair theoretician was content with what has been written about caste in the old scriptures and transmitted it to others with his seal of approval, the village sociologist found it difficult to digest. Even the very concept of caste required a definition. Controversy was raised as regards the status of this concept—is it to be treated as a cultural concept associated with pan-Indian civilization or is it to be regarded as a social structural category of universal application? Culturologists following the line of Indology opted for the former and sociologists for the latter. A seminal essay by Irawati Karve raising the question unambiguously, What is Caste? (1958) deserves special mention. Distinction between *varna, jati, gotra, vamsha* and the like assumed significance. The concept of subcaste came under heavy fire. Karve's concept of caste cluster found many followers. Mayer's (1960) distinction of kindred of cooperation and kindred of recognition as two facets of caste was quite attractive but was challenged by Yogesh Atal (1968). Atal strongly emphasized the need for distinguishing between caste as a unit (*jati*) and the caste system; using the notion of subset he provided a specific definition on the concept of subcaste. For the caste as a unit, Atal regards endogamy as the pivotal attribute; by the same token caste system is characterized by a plurality of interacting endogamous groups.

Other related concepts are those of dominant caste and caste hierarchy. The concept of dominant caste was proposed by M.N. Srinivas in his essay published in the *American Anthropologist* (1959). Soon it caught the fancy of many and became a catchword in rural sociology, as did his earlier concept of sanskritization. The concept of dominant caste was challenged by Brij Raj Chauhan (1967), Yogesh Atal (1968), S.C. Dube (1968), and T.K. Oommen (1970). In this connection, the concept of faction may be mentioned. In village studies in India, this was introduced by Oscar Lewis in his studies on group dynamics in a north Indian village (1958). While Lewis talked of permanent factions, which were kin-linked, and were cooperative in orientation, Yogesh Atal identified short-lived alliances as aspect of village factionalism, which he designated as ephemeral factions (Atal 1963, 1968). A number of scholars have written on the concept of faction, important among them being Ralph Nicholas (1965). K.N. Sharma introduced the concept of resource groups (1963, 1969).

A major motivating factor for village studies in the 1960s was the Community Development Programme (CDP). Several scholars went to the village to study the process of externally induced, directed, culture change. As a result, a number of case studies on innovation and innovators, and on leadership were written. These changed the focus of village studies from the description of social structure to social change. Some restudies have also been attempted: Wisers' *Behind Mudwalls (1961), and Ghurye's After a Century and Quarter–Lonikand: Then and Now* (1960) may be mentioned. Srinivas has revisited his legendary village of Rampura several times in past 20 years and is now writing for a book to be titled, *The Remembered Village.*

In more recent years, attention has shifted to a more general process of modernization. This has taken the scholars beyond the village. Employing more sophisticated tools either of survey research or of psychological testing, a group of villages have been taken up for investigation. There have been studies of communication links, flows of information, voting behavior, attitudes and aspirations, health practices and family planning, and of economic transactions in the village communities. Some have attempted to analyze class and power relations in a caste society, following largely the Weberian model (cf. Beteille, 1966).

There is, thus, a much more differentiated pattern of village studies in India. Of late, rural research in India has received a certain setback. The interest seems to be on the wane. Indian social science is increasingly getting oriented towards the urban. This shift in focus is understandable, although the neglect of the village cannot be commended.

It must be admitted that considerable data have been generated regarding the villages. There is a need to look at this data with a view to stocktaking. Most of this material is discrete, descriptive and discipline-specific. Very little has been done to consolidate and codify it. While methodological questions have been raised and debated, and concepts have been evolved and conceptual frameworks have been formulated, no rigorous writing on theory has appeared so far.

There is also a school of thought, which thinks in terms of creating a separate branch of rural social science in an interdisciplinary mould. One needs to raise a number of issues in this regard: (1) Can there be a rural social science as against an urban social science?; (2) Do we think of a unified social science or of individual disciplines developing rural specialisms—like rural economics, rural sociology, rural psychology, rural political science, and so on?; (3) If a separate rural social science is to be carved out, what shall be the core of such a discipline? Will it, for example, encompass all that obtains in the rural setting, or only that which is exclusively rural?; and (4) what should be the guiding principle for such a unification, and how to proceed?

All this is a tall task and would require very careful thinking. Even more important than the carving out of a rural social science is, in my view, the task of rejuvenating interest in village studies. There are several regions of the country from where not a single village has been reported professionally. Cross-subcultural studies of villages are also few. The question of generalization even at the level of a sub-cultural region has not been tackled adequately. The need for restudy of the villages, that were reported in 1950s is being felt—such studies would provide a diachronic frame and help assess change that has taken place during the interregnum.

Society's concern with the abolition of poverty, eradication of social discrimination and of untouchability, and with obliteration of illiteracy oblige the social scientist to commit himself to the study of those sectors where such evils are rampant. And these, no doubt, are largely in the rural areas where a majority of our population resides.

Giving up rural studies in favour of new fads and fashions in the profession is perhaps not a right thing to do. If rural sociology could flourish anywhere, it will be in places like India where the village is going to remain a key fact for quite some time.

Notes

1. Ramakrishan Mukherjee has enumerated these in his paper "On Village Studies in India" published in the *Indian Journal of Social Research* (Vol. IV, No. 2) 1963. He writes: "The Punjab Board of Economic Enquiry went on organizing village surveys conducted by individual workers (since 1920s). The Bengal Board of Economic Enquiry was set up and it undertook village surveys (1935); some in collaboration with the Indian Statistical Institute, Calcutta (Chakravarti, 1937). Tagore's Visva Bharati organized village surveys around Santiniketan, Bengal, under the auspices of the Visva Bharati Rural Reconstruction Board and at the individual initiative of Shri Kali Mohan Ghosh... Professors Bhattacharya and Natesan of Scottish Church College, Calcutta, published accounts of villages life in Bengal as collected by their students from respective villages (1932). The same was done by Professors Thomas and Ramakrishnan of Madras University (1940) with reference to the south Indian villages previously surveyed under the guidance of Gilbert Slater. The Cochin State published accounts of individual villages under the authorship of T.K. Sankara Menon (1935). Subramanian published the survey of south Indian village under the auspices of the Congress Economic and Political Studies (1936). Gujarat Vidyapeeth persuaded Prof. J.C. Kumarappa to undertake the survey of Matar Taluka in Gujarat (1931), and his work synchronized or was followed by those of G.C. Mukhtyar (1930), J.B. Shukla (1937), and others in Gujarat. Village surveys were also taken up in Maharashtra by the Gokhale Institute of Politics and Economics, Poona (Gadgil and Gadgil, 1940, and others). And so it went on with studies undertaken by organizations and by individuals themselves" (see Mukherjee in Desai 1969: 806).

2. It may, however, be noted in passing that Saksena has himself directed a village study for the Office of the Registrar General during 1961 census. Moreover, some of his Ph. D. students also carried out studies in single villages.

References

Atal, Yogesh, 1961, "Rural Studies: Indian Village" in *Eastern Anthropologist*, vol. 14, No. 3, pp. 249-257.

—, 1963, "Short lived Alliances as an Aspect of Factionalism in an Indian Village" in *The Journal of Social Sciences*, vol. 3, pp. 65-75.

—, 1968, *The Changing Frontiers of Caste*, National Publishing House, Delhi.

—, 1971, *Local Communities and National Polities*, National Publishing House, Delhi.

Bailey, F.G., 1957, *Caste and The Economic Frontier*, Manchester University Press, Manchester:.

Beteille, Andre, 1966, *Caste, Class and Power: Changing Patterns of Stratification in a Tanjore Village*, Oxford University Press, Bombay.

Bhattacharya, N.C. and L.A. Natesan (eds.), 1932, *Some Bengal Villages: Economic Survey*, University of Calcutta, Calcutta.

Bottomore, T.B., 1962, *Sociology: A Guide to Problems and Literature*, Allen and Unwin, London.

Carstairs, Morris B., 1957, *The Twice Born*, The Hogarth Press, London.

Chakravarti, N.C., 1937, *The Report on the Survey of Handloom Weaving Industry in Bengal*, Board of Economic Enquiry, Govt. of West Bengal, Calcutta.

Chauhan, Brij Raj, 1967, *A Rajasthan Village*, Associated Publishing House, New Delhi.

—, 1974, "Rural Studies" in *A Survey of Research in Sociology and Social Anthropology (ICSSR)*, Popular Prakashan, Bombay.

Desai, A.R. (ed.), 1969, *Rural Sociology in India*, Popular Prakashan, Bombay.

Dube, S.C., 1955, *Indian Village*, Routledge and Kegan Paul, London.

—, 1958a, *The Study of Indian Village Communities*. Presidential Address to the Social Anthropology Section, III All India Sociological Conference, Agra (Reprinted in Desai, Rural Sociology in India, pp. 790-95).

—, 1958b, *India's Changing Villages*, Routledge and Kegan Paul, London.

—, 1968, "Caste Dominance and Factionalism", *Contributions to Indian Sociology*, New Series No. II, pp. 58-81, Vikas Publishing House, Delhi.

Dumont, Louis and David Pocock, 1957, *Contributions to Indian Sociology*, No. 1 (pp. 7-22), Mouton and Co., The Hague.

Dumont, Louis, 1970, *Homo Hierarchicus: The Caste System and its Implications*, Wiedenfeld and Nicolson, London.

Gadgil, D.R. and V.R. Gadgil, 1940, *A Survey of Farm Business in Wai Taluka*, Gokhale Institute of Politics and Economics, Pune.

Ghurye, G.S., 1960, *After a Century and a Quarter: Lonikand Then and Now*, Popular Book Depot, Bombay.

Karve, Irawati, 1958, "What is Caste?", *Economic Weekly*, January-March-July, Vol.10.

Kumarappa, J.C., 1958, *Why the Village Movement* (sixth edition), Akhil Bharat Sarva Seva Sangh, Wardha.

—, 1961, *An Economic Survey of Matar Taluka*, Gujarat Vidyapeeth, Ahmedabad.

Lewis, Oscar, 1958, *Village Life in Northern India: Studies in a Delhi Village*, University of Illinois, Urbana.

Majumdar, D.N. (ed.), 1955, *Rural Profiles*, Ethnographic and Folk Culture Society, Lucknow.

—, 1958, *Caste and Communication in an Indian Village*, Asia Publishing House, Bombay.

Mandelbaum, David G., 1972, *Society in India*, Popular Prakashan, Bombay.

Marriott, McKim (ed.), 1955a, *Village India*, The University of Chicago Press, Chicago.

—, 1955b, "Little Communities in an Indigenous Civilization" in *Village India* (ed. Marriott), The University of Chicago, Chicago.

Martindale, Don, 1961, *Nature and Types of Sociological Theory*, Routledge and Kegan Paul, London.

Mathur, K.S., 1959, "Village Studies in India", *Man in India*, Vol. XXXIX, No.1, pp. 45-52.

Mayer, A.C., 1960, *Caste and Kinship in Central India*, Routledge and Kegan Paul, London.

Menon, T.K. Sankara, 1935, *Economic Survey of Nayerambalam Ernttampadi Antikkad*, Cochin State.

Mukherjee, G.C., 1930, *Life and Labour in a South Gujarat Village*, Bombay University, Bombay.

Mukherjee, Ramakrishna, 1958, *Six Villages of Bengal: A Socio-Economic Survey*, Asiatic Society, Calcutta.

Mukherjee, Ramakrishna, 1963 (Reprint 1969), "On Village Studies in India", *Indian Journal of Social Research*, Vol. IV, No.2, reprinted in *Rural Sociology in India* (ed. A.R. Desai, 1969), Popular Prakashan, Bombay, pp. 805-16.

Mukherjee, Ramakrishna and Monimohan Mukherjee, 1946, "A Note on the Concentration of Agricultural Wealth in Bengal, *Sankhya*, Vol. 7, Part 4.

Nicholas, Ralph, 1965, "Factions: a Comparative Analysis" in *Political Systems and the Distribution of Power* (ed. Michael Banton), Tavistock, London, pp. 21-61.

Oommen, T.K., 1970, "The Concept of Dominant Caste: Some Queries", *Contribution to Indian Sociology*, New Series No. 4, pp. 73-83.

Redfield, Robert, 1954, *Little Community*, Chicago University.

—, 1956, *Peasant Society and Culture*, Chicago University.

Rosser, Colin, 1955, "A Hermit Village in Kulu" in *India's Villages* (ed. M.N. Srinivas).

Saksena, R.N., 1959, Presidential Address, IV All India Sociological Conference, Calcutta.

Sharma, K.N., 1963, "Panchayat Leadership and Resource Group", *Sociological Bulletin*, Vol. 12, No. 1, pp. 47-52.

—, 1969, "Resource Networks and Resource Groups in Social Structure", *Eastern Anthropologist*, Vol. 22, No. 1, pp. 13-27.

Shukla, J.B., 1937, *Life and Labour in a Gujarat Taluka* (Olpad) Bombay University, Bombay.

Slater, Gilbert, 1918, *Some South Indian Villages*, Madras University Economic Series (1), Madras.

Srinivas, M.N., 1952, *Religion and Society among the Coorgs of South India*, Oxford University Press, Oxford.

—, (ed.), 1955, *India's Villages*, West Bengal Government Press, Calcutta.

—, 1956, "A Note on Sanskritization and Westernization", *The Far Eastern Quarterly*, Vol. 15, pp. 481-496.

—, 1959, "The Dominant Caste in Rampura", *American Anthropologist*, Vol. 61, pp. 1-16.

—, 1969, "The Village Studies and their Significance" in Desai, *Rural Sociology in India* (pp. 785-795) (reprinted from *Rural Profiles*, ed. Majumdar).

Sorokin, P.A. and C.C. Zimmerman, 1929, *Principle of Rural-Urban Sociology*, Henry Holt Co., New York.

Sorokin, P.A., C.C. Zimmerman and C.J. Galpin, 1930-32, *A Systematic Sourcebook in Rural Sociology* (3 vols.), University of Minnesota Press, Minneapolis.

Subramanian, N.S., 1936, *Survey of a South Indian Village*, Congress Economic Political Studies, No.2.

Thomas, P.J. and K.C. Ramakrishnan (eds.), 1940, *Some South Indian Villages: A Resurvey*, Madras University Economic Series (4), Madras.

Wiser, William H. and Charlotte Viall Wiser, 1951, *Behind Mudwalls*, Agricultural Mission, New York.

—, 1963, *Behind Mudwalls*, The University of California Press, Berkeley and Los Angeles.

9

Research Priorities in Anthropology

Anthropology in India could be viewed from two points: researches made and instructions imparted. While individual missionaries, government officials of the British administration and anthropologically oriented people began narrating the customs and ways of living of the tribal folk of India early enough, the recognition of the subject as a distinct discipline has been quite late. Even now not many universities in India impart instruction in anthropology and those which do so have only recently started; in fact some of the departments are not even a year old. The discipline itself is a new one in the field of knowledge and therefore is in a process of evolving itself. In the past few years, new dimensions have been discovered, new areas explored, and new approaches to the study attempted. With the introduction of anthropology in the university curricula, the "formative" stage of anthropology in India is over. This "constructive" stage requires us to critically estimate the researches done, carefully plan the further researches, and comparatively evaluate the courses of study. Some of the aspects which have hitherto received little attention and require urgent exploitation are discussed in the present paper.

I

Thinking "of the urgent tasks facing anthropological research in India" some eight years ago, Dube was reminded of Cecil Rhodes' words, "So little done, so much to do." He emphasized then that "to the anthropologist and social anthropologist the recording of the cultures of tribal and backward peoples is of primary importance" (1952:273). He further stressed the necessity of studying "tribal dialects, mythology and folklore, as well as tribal arts and crafts." While during the last decade there has been a "noticeable shift in the orientation and focus of interest" in the subject, and researches in rural India have been conducted, tribal research has received very little attention. All these aspects of study suggested by Dube in 1952 remain largely unexploited even today.

Indian anthropology is sometimes referred to as "unsystematic othnology." It is true that many tribal studies were done in the past because of the preoccupation of anthropologists with them, and the interests of other agencies. Several full length monographs on various tribes have been published. The number of papers and articles published in the research journals and popular periodicals is still greater. We have a richness of othnographic detail. But have we attempted any elaborate comparisons to give coherence and synthesis to the vastly scattered data? The queerness of the customs of a people may be interesting reading but they become significant and meaningful for the social anthropologist only when they are put to a rigorous scientific analysis and comparative treatment. Many back numbers of various journals are not accessible to every student and many of the monographs have gone out of print. Many of the available old monographs are either travelogues or written with emotional attachments. Moreover, they lack theoretical depth and methodological sophistication. The forces and factors of change have also affected tribal societies; the impacts and consequences of culture-contact demand re-study and further enquiry. The problems of administration and the introduction of modern facilities into these areas raise many significant questions of applied anthropology. In brief, the following attempts may be suggested:

1. The neglected aspects of tribal life like mythology, dialect, folklore, arts and crafts may be taken up for study. Similarly those tribes, which have not so far been studied may also be investigated soon so that their ways of living may be recorded before it is too late.
2. Some library researches should also be conducted to accomplish the following tasks:
    a. To compile the vastly scattered material in order to prepare a compendium on the model of "our primitive contemporaries" (Murdock, 1934).
    b. Some research towards comparisons of various institutions and societies may also be attempted.
    c. A comprehensive bibliography of the available material and its sources in a chronological sequence about each society may be prepared for ready reference. The lead in this direction has been given by David G. Mandelbaum.
    d. Any work along Yale University "area-files" will also be extremely useful.
3. Many of the othnographies have been written in a traditional manner. As descriptions they are excellent but viewed as a contribution to the body of theory, they will perhaps bear a rigorous scrutiny. The development of research techniques and the emphasis on specialization have made it imperative to conduct re-studies. Speaking strictly, in terms of the years that have lapsed, since those studies were made, it will be rewarding indeed to evaluate the changing patterns of the tribal life in a diachronic frame of reference.
4. The contacts of the tribes with the neighbouring peasantry have given rise to a sort of tribe-peasant continuum. This continuum should be studied from a comparative point of view. Surajit Sinha's paper entitled "Tribal Cultures of India as a Dimension of Little Tradition in the Study of Indian Civilization: A Preliminary Statement" (1957) and

Martin Orans' (1959) paper on the processes of solidarity-emulation among Santals represent the type of researches done in this direction. But they are only first steps and much remains to be done.

5. Problems arising out of the introduction of modern facilities in tribal areas by the government or other philanthropic agencies can provide a good material for building up case studies. These will illustrate the utility and applicability of anthropological knowledge in the administration of these areas.

II

Much attention in the last decade has been focussed on rural research. Many anthropologists, Indian and foreign, have worked in the village communities and contributed to our understanding of Indian society. While this has been a significant shift, good for the advancement of our science, there are many who adhere to the traditional norms of the subject and refuse to accept the changing situation. To them, social anthropology is the study of tribes. If anthropology is to be understood as the science of Man and his activities, it will be necessary for us to justify the definition by taking into our scope of study Man at all levels of culture. Denial of this responsibility will be suicidal for the subject. Even to say that this field belongs to other social sciences will not suffice. The fact remains that most of the rural studies carried out in India in the recent years are by anthropologists. We should not disown our own contribution. Researches in the rural areas by an anthropologist are not an encroachment on others' field but a natural and logical extension of his own field of study. The tools of research that we sharpened in the microcosm of a tribal society could easily and most effectively be used in consonance and conjunction with the tools of other social sciences in the village community. In this age where tight walls of different disciplines are breaking down and an interdisciplinary approach is promulgated, rural India provides a good meeting ground for the social sciences interested in the study of the village. The anthropologist like the staunch believer of the Trobriander's code of reciprocity should welcome this happy "merging".

Looking to the vastness of this subcontinent the number of studies done is quite meagre. Many regional variations in the structure and organization of the village community will have to be recorded to get a clear perspective of an "ideal type" of village in India. Various linkages of the "part-society" with the "whole" of which it is a "part" are also to be assessed on a comparative base. In the post-independence era, the pace of planned culture change has been greatly accelerated. This requires us to record the existing situations and structure of the society, and also to examine and evaluate the processes, problems and products of change. Some of the broad areas that may be covered by our researches in the near future are enumerated below:

1. Full length monographic studies of various villages in the different parts of the country may be encouraged. These will provide the "benchmark data" which are a preliminary requisite for any conscientious planner. Apart from their practical value in the immediate present, such studies will be invaluable records of the existing rural social structure which is undergoing rapid changes. It will also help in bringing out the relevant points that contribute to the "representativeness" of the Indian village.
2. Though we have not reached a stage when plans for re-studies could be initiated, it is desired that comparative studies of village communities or of their various institutions be started. In order to trace out the range of similarities and differences between different villages, and to find out the ramifications of various institutions in the region or nation, a comparative approach seems to be essential. It is, therefore, necessary that comparative microscopic studies of village communities be made or

hypotheses arrived at through such studies be subjected to demonstrability through microscopic studies of a comparative nature. Such comparative studies, for purposes of classification, could be placed in two categories: comparisons of the communities; and comparisons of an institution in various communities. For the first category, the following types of comparisons may be suggested:

(a) Diachronic study of the same community.
(b) Study of more than one village in the same culture-area (region).
(c) Study of more than one village in different culture-areas (regions).
(d) Comparisons between a small village, large village, town and city in the same region and in different regions.

Similarly, for the second category the following types of comparisons may be suggested:

(a) Functioning of an institution in village communities of the same culture-area (region).
(b) Functioning of an institution in different culture-areas (regions).
(c) Functioning of an institution in a small village, large village, town and city of the same region and of different regions.

In the context of caste, it will be fruitful to distinguish between *a* caste and *the* caste. The former refers to an institution, while the latter to the system of working of many castes. The concept of "dominant caste" as propounded by Srinivas will have to be extended so as to cover the region. Similarly, in assessing the changing frontiers of caste, comparative studies will bear more fruitful results. Studies in inter-village leadership and inter-village panchayat also emphasize the need for a comparative approach. Similarly, a concept of the "dominant village" could also be developed. To define in more precise terms the concept of "region" in the sociological sense, comparative study is the only method to be followed.

3. Studies in social and cultural change have been done in the country. Attention will have to be concentrated on specific problems and attempts at building up good case studies on the pattern of the Spicer edited volume or Paul edited volume will be of great service to the action oriented administrator and his agents of communication in rural areas. They will also serve as "instructional aids" in training development personnel. Dube's *India's Changing Villages* serves as an excellent example of a study conducted with a view to evaluating the programmes of the CDP in western Uttar Pradesh.

IV

The results of research enrich the body of the theory. The advancements in theory are reflected in the syllabi of university instruction. The author who observed in 1952 that "recording the cultures of tribal and backward peoples is of primary importance (Dube, 1958:273) for the social anthropologist," revised his statement in 1958 by observing that "anthropologists are no longer concerned primarily or mainly with the study of tribal cultures..." and that "there has been a noticeable shift in the orientation and focus of interest". In the light of recent developments in the subject and greater specialization in its various branches, it will be good to critically evaluate whether our courses of study have been able to keep pace with them or whether they are still lagging behind.

It has to be accepted that the age of general anthropology is over. The growing specialization demands greater concentration on any one branch of it. It will be unjust to load a student of physical anthropology with many papers on social anthropology and vice versa; for that will amount to a diversion from, and a neglect of, some of the important aspects of the main branch of specialization.

An enquiry into the syllabi of various universities imparting instruction in anthropology can form the base of a separate paper altogether. In such an enquiry it will be good if the following questions are answered:

1. Whether our courses of study have been able to cope with the recent developments in the subject.
2. Whether our instructions aim at specialization in any branch of the subject or they tend to be of a "general" type.
3. How much specialization have we been able to achieve?
4. What changes and shifts do we require in our courses of study?
5. In which direction should our researches be channelized?

References

Dube, S.C., 1952, "The Urgent Tasks of Anthropology in India Today" in *Actes du Ivec Congress International des Sciences Anthropologioues et Ethnologioues*, Vienne 1952, Tome III (Public 1956).

Dube, S.C., 1958, *The Study of Indian Village Communities*. Presidential Address, Social Anthropology Section, Indian Sociological Conference, Agra.

Dube, S.C., 1958, *India's Changing Villages*, Routledge and Kegan Paul, London.

Lewis, Oscar, 1956, "Comparisons in Cultural Anthropology" in *Current Anthropology* (ed. W.L. Jr. Thomas), Chicago.

Murdock, G.P., 1934, *Our Primitive Contemporaries*, The Macmillan Company, New York.

Majumdar, D.N., 1947, "Indian Anthropology through the Decades" in *Matrix of Indian Culture*, Lucknow.

Orans, M., 1959, "A Tribe in Search of a Great Tradition: The Emulation-Solidarity Conflict," *Man in India*, Vol. 39, No. 2.

Paul, Benjemin D. (ed.), 1955, *Health Culture and Community*, Russel Sage Foundation, New York.

Sinha, Surajit, 1957, "Tribal Cultures of Peninsular India as a Dimension of Little Tradition in the Study of Indian Civilization: A Preliminary Statement", *Man in India*, Vol. 37. No. 2.

Spicer, E.H. (ed.), 1952, *Human Problems in Technological Change*, Russel Sage Foundation, New York.

Srinivas, M.N. (ed.), 1955, "Introduction" in *India's Villages*, West Bengal Government.

Srinivas, M.N., 1959, "The Dominant Caste in Rampura", *American Anthropologist*, Vol. 61. No. 1.

10

Research Priorities in Education*

Social scientists in India have not paid sufficient attention to the field of education. Barring economists—who have focussed on the issue of financing of education and on the relationship between education and economic development—there is very little contribution by other social sciences in understanding the core problems of Indian education. Similarly, educationists—those belonging to the discipline of education—have also neglected research on the social science aspects of education. They have primarily focussed on the conventional kind of educational research in the narrow precincts of the educational subsystem. There is, thus, a need to encourage social scientific research on education, building up on whatever has been done in the past and responding to the challenges of the day.

It must, however, be acknowledged that Indian social science has gradually moved towards interdisciplinary research in recent years. Some social science departments in the universities, and research institutes set up outside of the university system—particularly under the aegis of the Indian Council of Social Science Research—have taken up interdisciplinary and problem-oriented research projects, including in the field of education. In this regard, particular

* This is a report on a meeting of experts organized at the Indian Institute of Education, Pune in 1998 to draw an agenda for research on education. The author was then Director-General of the Institute.

mention may be made of the two major projects carried out under the sponsorship of NCERT and ICSSR in the late 1960s and early 1970s. These have become landmarks in the history of educational research as they involved a large number of social scientists and pioneered work in the field of sociology of education.

The NCERT exercise was attempted to provide the needed data on various aspects of education to the Kothari Commission set up by the Government of India to review the system of education in India and to provide guidelines for future. The ICSSR study attempted to measure the impact of educational privileges offered to students belonging to the scheduled castes and scheduled tribes in 18 different states of India. This project was undertaken at the behest of the Ministry of Home Affairs, Government of India. The outcome of these two exercises resulted in some noteworthy research publications.

But these are discrete and disparate studies. They did not lead either to any continuous programme of research on education, or to the consolidation of the findings to be of use to policy makers and planners.

This situation needs to be remedied. It may require an investigation into the causes of lack of interest and motivation among social scientists to carry out such research so that a suitable climate is created to promote research in this vital area of national importance.

Need for Prioritization

Standing on the threshold of the 21st century, and still struggling with the enormous task of (i) eradicating illiteracy that characterizes more than 40 per cent of our population; (ii) universalizing primary education; and (iii) responding to the demand for continuing education, India offers a veritable ground for empirical research on various aspects of education.

More than that, the society expects the social sciences to participate in the campaign on "Education for All" and to help prepare a blueprint for the "learning society" of the future. Social scientists are called upon to engage in research and reflection on several issues relative to education in India.

Where to begin? If so much remains to be done, what is it that ought to be done on a priority basis? And, who should determine the priorities? There is a danger that in our enthusiasm to promote educational research we may dissipate our limited resources—human and financial—in carrying out "non-relevant", and even "esoteric" research. Obviously, we cannot afford such a luxury. We have, therefore, to carefully examine as to where we stand and in what direction we have to proceed.

The task of drawing up a do-able agenda is not easy. With a virtually unexplored territory, there are several competing candidates for inclusion in the inventory of topics for research. The identification of topics by any individual or a group of persons is guided by several considerations: theoretical and disciplinary orientation; availability and accessibility of data; state of methodological sophistication, including the penetration of computer culture; ideological predilections; and individual idiosyncrasies. In the Indian context, it is also of crucial importance that the state continues to be the principal fund-giver for social science research; as such the donor's perception of relevance assumes special significance. In fixing priorities, not only the interests of the producer of research but also the demands of the donor and the needs of the end-user —that is, the consumers of research—will have to be kept in view. A do-able agenda for research will be one that matches the societal and statal demands with the scientific capabilities to respond to the challenge.

The concepts of education and relevance need to be defined. Taking a very broad view, education may include the entire process of socialization and enculturation through which cultural heritage is transmitted from one generation to another, and the young of the society are inducted into the culture. But such processes operate in all societies—pre-literate, non-literate, semi-literate and literate. And, then, education is defined by many as not only the process of transmission of already existing knowledge, but also of generation of new knowledge and a harbinger of change. Moreover, there are changing definitions of literacy—for example, the arrival of computers has created a new cadre of incomputerates. Thus, to the traditional three R's, computeracy has been added as a component of literacy and has been made a prime focus of life-long, continuing education. On the other hand, the outreach of the audio-visual media is making literacy redundant for acquiring new knowledge or forming opinions and attitudes. In this manner, even the very definition of the concept of education has become a researchable question.

The definition of relevance is similarly problematic as different actors from their respective vantage points can variously define relevance. What is regarded as relevant by one set of actors may be regarded as irrelevant by others. In the absence of a consensus on relevance, it may not be easy to arrive at a common list of priority themes for research. Assigning space for the "odd man out" a list of priorities will have to include those themes on which there is general agreement.

Even after overcoming the definitional crisis a prioritizing exercise has to delimit the scope in terms either of the (1) target areas or populations; or (2) aspects of education—policy, pedagogy, student clientele, teaching profession, management, financing etc. Alongside investigating the educational scene, the thinking community may also like to reflect on the role of education and even the alternative ways of responding to the growing demand for literacy, education, and skill training.

The Agenda

Keeping all these constraints in view, the expert group has suggested an agenda for promoting social science research on education in India. It has identified (1) the needs for strengthening the social science infrastructure; (2) the topics to be researched on a priority basis; and (3) the strategies for the effective utilization of research findings in policy making and planning.

Interventions to Strengthen Social Science Infrastructure

To promote social science research on education, it is necessary to train young researchers from various social science disciplines in the methodology of research—including the use of computers and statistical analysis—and to orient them to the field of social science of education. Such training will also be needed for those working in the faculties of teacher training colleges. Short-term training and orientation courses may be planned for this purpose.

There is also the need to do the stock-taking of already existing research on education relative to India—to review achievements of the past and to identify the gaps, the failures, and the neglected areas. Secondly, there is need to consolidate and systematize our theoretical gains and methodological innovations. The material generated through such an exercise will be useful for training and orientation both of the young and new researchers.

Areas of Priorities for Research

General Issues for Reflection and Research

1. Where has the education system failed and why? This will require reviewing the past policies and drawing the emergent educational profile. Based on the secondary data and findings of previously carried out studies such research will help in analyzing the factors responsible for the current state of affairs and in suggesting ways and means to alleviate the situation. Such research should also focus on the impact of linguistic policy on educational performance. The twin

relationship between education and development—that is, development influencing education and education impacting on development—provides a useful theme for research. Such studies would attempt to empirically test the assumed relationship between the two variables and also to see whether education provides a solution to all kinds of developmental problems or is itself part of the problem. Of particular importance will be to examine the relationship between education and poverty, education and employment, and employment and poverty. These researches will contribute to the fulfilment of the international commitment for the eradication of poverty and promotion of social development.

2. Role of education in the inculcation of values: ethical/moral and democratic. This is an area both for research and reflection. The desirability of value education is a matter of choice and needs to be debated. That debate should, however, be guided by an analysis of the current content of education from the point of view of values and assess their impact on the educated. What is the value profile of the educated compared to those of the uneducated, and which group is the problematic? Moreover, what costs are involved, compared to what gains, if teaching is to be heavily biased towards value inculcation? Is there compatibility between democratic values and education? [There is a view that education creates strata and inequalities—knowledge inequalities leading to income inequalities and further to status inequalities whereas democracy is premised on equality.] How are the two contrasting value syndromes to be accommodated in a single process? How does education prepare a person to be a good and informed citizen? The latter question will require studies of the role of education in the process of political socialization.
3. How should the task of universalization of primary education be handled? Should primary education be the

sole responsibility of the state or should the present system of public schools (particularly English medium schools) be allowed to continue? What about the coexistence of the traditional schools (e.g., *Vaidic Pathshalas* and *Madarsas*) which cater to other specific needs and follow a different system of learning? The phenomenon of child labour, and promotion of education among them, needs to be carefully examined keeping in view its short-term and long-term consequences on the family and society.

The question of age at which a child should enter the primary school also deserves to be examined both in terms of its pedagogical desirability, and the carrying capacity on the school system. The consequences on the family time-budget for looking after children, in case of raising the school entrance age, will also have to be assessed.

4. Review of the current examination system and the possible alternatives with an estimation of their economic, social and administrative costs is another area that deserves priority attention.
5. How to prepare the Indian education system to respond to the processes of globalization, liberalization and privatization? The study of these processes need to be carried out in a futuristic perspective, identifying the impending demands on the education system, calculating the costs involved in meeting them and suggesting the reformation of the system to handle the new demand structure.

Empirical Studies: Investigating the Current Educational Scene

1. The Problem of unequal access to education: Systematic empirical studies are needed in different parts of the country to identify the causes that have denied access to education to women and girls, certain caste and tribal groups, poverty-stricken strata, and to people in remote areas. To meet the goal of "reaching the unreached" these

studies are expected not only to analyze the factors but also to suggest strategies to promote access to education. Any innovations carried out by the NGOs in this area should provide good material for case studies.

2. Distribution of public expenditure on education: Who benefits from public expenditure for education? Who shares financial responsibility? Systematic studies are needed on sources of funds for education at different levels and their implications for the quality of education. In particular, relative effectiveness of alternative methods of funding such as, fees, loans, community financing, external financing vs. state financing, needs to be carefully analyzed. Implications of the governmental decision to spend 6 per cent of the GDP on education, should also be worked out. Another area for research is the growing phenomenon of capitation fees leading to the commercialization of education, on the one hand, and denial of access to merited but poor students, on the other.
3. The phenomenon of surrogate schools: Over the years, several private enterprises have sprung up, particularly in metropolitan towns, to prepare students for admission into professional institutions, as well as to impart training in the use of computers, business management and similar other skills. While not always satisfying the eligibility criteria, these institutions are too much in demand as is evident from the growing size of their clientele. In what ways do they supplement the role of the formally recognized institutions, and how do they pose a challenge to them? Can these unplanned structures—as part of the "informal sector"—be helped to improve their performance so that their contribution to human resource development be acknowledged and better ensured?
4. Mismatch between educational qualifications and occupational needs: Is the content of education related to new opportunities and challenges in the society: at primary

level in technical subjects, e.g., engineering, in other degree courses?

5. Burgeoning demand for higher education and the system's response: Over the years, the demand for higher education has been rising and the system is finding it difficult to accommodate all the aspiring candidates. The severity of examinations has, on the one hand, generated a good deal of wastage (in terms of high rates of failures) and, on the other, increased competition among those who pass out—the high percentage of marks required for admission by the institutions—is causing frustration among many. What happens to those who fail an examination (its impact on the family, on the personality of the student, and the institution which has to re-accommodate the repeaters), and what options are left for those who clear the examination but are unable to enter into an institution of higher learning because of limited number of seats? This is a serious problem and needs to be investigated in different states of the country so that proper policy measures can be initiated.
6. Systematic case studies of educational innovations and experiments currently being conducted in the country are needed to assess the feasibility of their replication and nation-wide adoption.
7. Action research is indicated in the following areas: (a) empowerment of local people for demanding better education services; (b) developing effective systems at the primary level; and (c) school mapping and location of schools to increase access.
8. Within the school system, researches on the following themes deserve priority attention:
   (a) Selection and admission of students.
   (b) Teachers as role models.
   (c) Monitoring teaching-learning process in formal educational institutions.

   (d) Quality of textbooks and effectiveness of textbook committees.
   (e) Work culture in educational institutions.
   (f) Relevance and content of focus of "area studies" in higher education.
   (g) Sports education.
9. Other topics for research:
   (a) Comparative study of primary and vocational education in India and in industrially advanced countries.
   (b) Researches on various facets of non-formal education including its relationship with formal systems of learning, continuing education, and the potential for expansion—is it complementary or a replacement alternative? What costs are involved if non-formal is to replace the formal?
   (c) Research on schools for minorities (particularly Muslim and tribal schools).
   (d) Schools as private enterprises and their management.
   (e) Child labour and education.
   (f) Re-examination of the three language formula from the viewpoint of national needs and local socio-cultural implications; aberrations in planning and implementation of the three language formula, corrective measures; training needs of teaching second and third languages as distinct from first and second language teaching.

Ensuring Utilization of Research Findings

To quote from OECD report on Utilization of the Social Sciences in Policy Making (1977):

> The social sciences cannot be considered simply as instruments for administrative management; nor is their policy relevance confined to some residual area of concerns labelled 'social policy'.

> The social impact of social sciences is, therefore, not limited to their direct utilization by public authorities. In their attempt to describe and analyze social reality more effectively, they provide the individual with deeper insights into his community and, conversely, contribute to mould the ways in which the community sees itself.

It is recognized that while the social scientists complain about the non-utilization of their research findings by the policy makers and planners, the latter generally hint at the non-utilizability of these research writings because of their being written in esoteric, and so-called "jargonated" language, or being overly algebraic in presentation. But when a research is carried out on a "relevant" topic, and is also funded by the end-user, there are better chances of utilization of its findings.

Utilization of research results is itself an area of research. It is recommended that research be undertaken to find out where social sciences have contributed to policy making in India, and on what fronts research findings have remained unutilized. The identification of factors that have helped or hindered the use of social science research for policy, or for public debate will be an excellent area for research.

Additionally, it is recommended that ways be found to establish dialogue between the producers of research and its consumers.

Timely publication of research reports, dissemination of their main findings in the language intelligible to the user, and occasional organization of discussion for involving social scientists, educationists, people from administration and the public must receive priority attention so that relevant research is not only carried out by the social scientists but is also put to good societal use.

Epilogue

This agenda has been drawn collectively by a group of scholars belonging to different academic institutions and representatives of ICSSR, NCERT, and NIEPA, all of whom are committed to the cause of furthering social science research on education. It is hoped that this document will not only guide their future plans and activities but also encourage other social scientists and research institutions to draw upon this resource and take initiative to plan research in the area of education and contribute to the national cause of promoting education for all.

The topics suggested here are those that the workshop participants regarded as relevant and deserving of priority attention. They are general in their scope leaving ample freedom for the researchers to delimit and sharpen the focus for investigation. Students registered for M.Phil. or for Ph.D. may take up these studies. These can also be taken up by senior scholars individually or as a team, and even by a group of interested research institutions in a cross-cultural comparative framework.

The issues raised for reflection may be discussed in seminars and workshops, or may be taken up for sustained and prolonged debate and discussion by a think-tank within an organization, or so constituted by any agency involving eminent people from different organizations to meet at regular intervals.

More important is the need to train the young researchers both in the social science of education and in the methodology of social science research. In addition, efforts are needed to create a good documentation centre and a data bank on education. The Indian Institute of Education is already taking steps in this direction.

11

Social Transformation: The Indian Context*

You have done me honour by inviting me to deliver the keynote address. For me, this is a special occasion as I come back to this university from where I began my teaching career in 1960; in fact, I had the privilege of initiating teaching of social anthropology here. That was the year when sociology teaching was also started. But the departments were distanced from each other—anthropology belonged to the faculty of science and sociology to the faculty of arts. Social anthropologists, like me, had indeed a very hard time being sandwiched between sociologists and the physical anthropologists, both regarding them as non-members to their ilk. While sociologists regarded social anthropologists as "intruders" in their cherished territory, physical anthropologists considered the new genre of social anthropologists as "converts" to the new faith of sociology.

Both the disciplines were at that time struggling to gain recognition in the Indian academe. In those days, these disciplines were taught only in a few universities. Only the newly created universities such as this university took the

* Keynote address given at the National Seminar on Social Transformation of Indian Society: The Post-Independence Era, organized by Department of Sociology, Punjab University, Chandigarh, on 9 March, 2000.

initiative to introduce them, while the old universities remained largely indifferent to their introduction. The first head of sociology at this university was a product of Lucknow where, curiously enough, both sociology and anthropology were introduced in the department of economics; they earned their separate existence only in the first years of our independence. The successor head of sociology here was a graduate from Bombay University where the sociology-anthropology combine emerged from the studies of Indology and urban geography. Even today, Bombay does not have a separate department of anthropology, and in Lucknow, little interaction exists between the two departments. When Delhi University started a separate department of sociology, it hired Professor Srinivas—a product of Bombay and Oxford—who was acclaimed as a social anthropologist, but he remained distanced from the older department of anthropology in the same university. The first reader-head of the department of anthropology at the Panjab University was from Delhi where physical anthropology reigned supreme; he was also averse to the idea of social anthropologists coming closer to sociologists. I was, however, lucky in having good relations with our sociology colleagues who even asked me to conduct classes in kinship and in rural sociology. Some of the sociology students accompanied me to the field visits in the nearby village of Daddu Majra.

Struggling to gain recognition and establish separate identities, the practitioners of both the disciplines—particularly the hardliners—were engaged in carving out their specific emphases and orientations. While anthropology focussed on the tribes, sociology concentrated on general theory of society and on Indological studies based on texts and scriptures. However, both the disciplines were engaged in the portrayal of the Indian social structure. Indological studies of the type Ghurye and his followers pursued presented ideal-typical features of the Indian (read Hindu) society, and anthropological studies were in the nature of ethnographies written in the idiom of eternal present. This was a continuation of the trend initiated by the Britishers during the colonial era. They were interested in the queer and exotic, and were eager to prove the superiority of their culture. In the post-independence era, Indian society became the research site for anthropologists from other countries of the West, particularly the United States. It was quite in tune with the definition of the discipline of anthropology as the "study of 'other' societies, as against sociology which studied the societies of its practitioners. Strangely, in India, both sociologists and anthropologists were studying their own society, making the fine distinction between them superfluous. For example, it made little sense to regard the study of caste by Hutton as anthropology, and Ghurye's work on caste as sociology. And yet, academic debates in the 1950s and 1960s in India hinged on this issue of distinguishing between anthropology and sociology. I recall a professor of sociology complimenting me on my intervention in a national conference mistaking me as a sociologist. When he learnt that I was trained as an anthropologist he expressed his astonishment. To my query as to how did it matter, he remarked: Oh! There is a difference; your discipline begins with A, and sociology with an S. To this I quipped: But sir! Both end with 'Y'. Sure, he was not amused. I also told my enthusiastic head that if physical anthropology could go down to the study of Lemurs and Langurs, why is he opposed to the idea of social anthropologists going up to the villages and towns. But he remained adamant. I therefore, took the first opportunity to bid him goodbye when Agra University offered me a position in sociology.

The fact that you chose this anthropologist to inaugurate the seminar hopefully signals that the days of that fruitless debate are now over. The watertight compartmentalization of knowledge is a thing of the past. Interdisciplinarity is the needed orientation particularly when we discuss the issue of development and change.

This brief excursion to the past of our disciplines gives me a good launching pad to comment on the theme of this seminar. I wish to underline the fact that concern with change in Indian sociology is rather recent and that it has been responsible for bringing the two specialties closer to each other. In the initial phases of the growth of the twin disciplines in India, the focus was not on change. It was on the depiction of Indian society. Even when the post-independent India initiated programmes of socio-cultural change in a planned manner, the leadership in the profession showed its keenness to record the present lest things may change and we lose the opportunity to research and report on existing social structures.

It was the introduction of the Community Development Programmes in India, with focus on rural development, which led Indian sociologists and anthropologists to study the village communities. Anthropologists found this as a legitimate extension of their scope; for, the technique of ethnographic investigation suited the study of the villages. Urban sociologists also found merit in the study of the villages to better understand the dynamics of rural-urban interactions. The village thus became a common meeting ground for the Indian sociologists and anthropologists. Three major works published in the year 1955 mark a turning point in Indian sociology; these were S.C. Dube's *Indian Village*; M.N. Srinivas' edited volume titled *India's Villages;* and Mckim Marriott's edited volume on *Village India.* Incidentally, all the three scholars were anthropologists. These works provided the much-needed Indian flavour to A.R. Desai's elementary textbook on *Rural Sociology,* which had very little Indian in it. But in all these studies, change was not the prime focus. They, however, provided an alternative to what Srinivas had described "the book view and the upper caste view" of Indian society. But they were not studies in (change: only by inference one could locate the changes—those elements that seem to depart from the ideal-typical. If change is regarded as difference between two points of time—T1 and T2—then these studies could best be regarded as T1 studies to be compared with later T2 studies.

Concern with change, thus, figured in the studies of that era only marginally. Change was seen in the context of idealized past. But the increasing attention to community development helped change our orientation to change. We moved from orientation to past to orientation to the present. Rather than comparing change in a T1-T2 framework, change was compared between one society and the other at the same time locus—between S1 and S2 at T1 or T2. It was not insignificant that while Dube's *Indian Village* ended with a chapter on change in the Shamirpet village, his 1958 book was fully devoted to *India's Changing Villages* being the study of villages in the state of Uttar Pradesh covered by the Community Development Programme. He focussed on the changes introduced in a planned manner and analyzed cultural and social factors responsible for their selective acceptance or rejection. Studies of change carried out during that phase were in fact studies of "non-change". Researchers carried out studies to find out as to why people did not accept an innovation. And the reasons for such rejection were located in the tradition and culture; the argument advanced by the social scientists was that any programme of directed culture change must give due regard to social and cultural factors to avoid costly failures.

It is this emphasis on "tradition" that led to a shift in our studies of social change. If in the first phase, change was defined as departure from the past-real or ideal-typical, the second phase focussed on the analysis of "resistance to change" paving way for the third phase that related to the investigation of the broader processes of change under the rubric "modernization" in which the developed West became our positive reference group. Thus, we moved from the analysis of orthogenetic change—change from within, to exogenous change—change from without. And ultimately, our focus covered both these processes. Scholars wrote about folk-urban continuum, debated the dichotomy between tradition and modernity, and then engaged in the analysis of various processes of change—urbanization, industrialization, universalization of education, citizen participation in a democratic polity, and so on. Much broader, micro issues such as economic and political development, nation-building and national integration became the favoured topics for research. As our orientations changed, our fields of study also became different. Today, there are very few who study the tribes or the villages. More and more people are getting interested in the urban studies and the wider processes, and focussing more on themes than on communities.

All this has brought about yet another shift in the studies of change. In this new phase change is seen in the context of future. From the mid-1970s when we realized the fast approaching Y2K—the year 2000, our mode of thinking got transformed. As elsewhere in the world, the magic figure of 2000 led scholars to review the past performance of development for preparing a balance sheet of achievements and failures; but more than that, it also encouraged them to think and predict the future. Willy-nilly all became votaries of the new emerging discipline of futurology. These exercises not only predicted the likely future and gave future shocks—to borrow the title of Alvin Toffler's book—but also prompted many to draw blueprints of desirable futures. The concern was to see how societies would be transiting to the new millennium and what social transformations have already occurred and what more are expected or engineered. Distinctions were made between changes that are inevitable, or are possible if not checked and the desirable.

In this regard, the collapse of Communism and the disintegration of the Soviet Union provided a new impetus. The changing societies of Eastern Europe came to be described as economies in transition—transition from a communist mode to a capitalist mode, from dictatorial-totalitarian regimes to democratic forms of government. For such drastic and radical changes, the word change appeared to be rather inadequate. This is how the word "social transformation" became the key phrase to capture the new manifestation of change worldwide.

UNESCO—the only body within the United Nations system that has specific mandate to promote social sciences—decided to launch a major programme on social change similar to a programme in the natural sciences called Man and the Biosphere—MAB. Some suggested that the new social science programme be called MAS or Man and the Sociosphere. There were other lengthy nomenclatures suggested at the international meeting held to launch the programme, but such names did not yield a good acronym. As UNESCO's Regional Adviser for Asia and the Pacific, I was party to all this dialogue, and had in fact, carried out a survey among leading social scientists of the region to obtain their views on the thrust of the UNESCO programme. It is on record that I pleaded for calling this programme, Management of Social Transformations, acronymed as MOST. When people showed their reluctance, I simply said that social sciences receive the LEAST by way of funding from the UNESCO's overall budget; we must, therefore, make the MOST out of it. That pun worked. And now MOST is a well-known acronym in social sciences.

Those who opposed the coinage of MOST had two major difficulties. They were afraid that emphasis on social transformation would limit the scope of their enquiry to fewer aspects of social change and development. Also they expressed the fear that the international community, and particularly UNESCO will "manage" the change, rather than study it; such intervention in their view was uncalled for, and even undesirable. While such suspicion still lurks, the activities of MOST carried out so far have given ample proof that these fears were unfounded. The idea was not to manage, but to study how societies are managing their social transformations. It is the process of social transformation, including its management, that is the focus of UNESCO's programme.

There is another development that should also be mentioned. At the international level, United Nations organized a series of international conferences and summits to mark the 50th anniversary of the founding of the United Nations, and also to chart out an agenda for the coming millennium. All these conferences that culminated in the World Summit for Social Development in 1995 in Copenhagen, Denmark critically reviewed the past development of our societies and came to the conclusion that despite achievements on the economic front, there is a big deficit in the social sector, and a growing environmental crisis. The Summit recommended that the new development must be people-centred, and must address the problems of social development particularly, the problem of eradication of poverty, of creating productive employment, and curbing tendencies toward social disintegration. The Summit agreed that while there are common problems there cannot be common solutions in the face of uncommon opportunities that exist. We need to think globally but will have to act locally, trying to find solutions that are culture-specific and society relevant. This was also an indirect acknowledgement of the failure of our development paradigm that was premised on a universal panacea: that which worked in the North will also cure the ailment of the South.

This became apparent after the collapse of Communism in Eastern Europe. Thinking that rapid social transformation of these countries into a capitalist mode will improve the situation, the steps that the leaders of these countries took led only to frustration. Highlighting this feature, the International Commission on Peace and Food, headed by Professor M.S. Swaminathan, wrote (1994:134):

> The actual results were quite contrary to the expectations of these countries...The initial phase of reforms had a disastrous impact on the economies, on the people, and in some countries on peace and

> political stability. From 1990 to 1993, production in all 25 nations declined drastically, from a minimum of 10 per cent in Poland, 20 per cent in Hungary and 22 per cent in the Czech Republic to a maximum of 45 per cent in Russia, 57 per cent in Latvia, and 75 per cent in Armenia. Investment fell by an average rate of 13-14 per cent per year from 1990 to 1992, and by a three-year total of more than 50 per cent in Russia. The fall in real incomes followed that of output, and the impact was made even more severe, especially for pensioners, by the simultaneous dismantling of the vast social support system and dramatic increase in the cost of essential consumer goods. The drastic decline in living standards for the vast majority has been accompanied by the emergence of a new class of instantaneous millionaires...inflation in most of these countries gained tremendous momentum as the reforms proceeded....The tremendous physical and psychological stress experienced by people in the region as a result of the economic collapse is reflected in the sharp fall in birth rates and the steep rise in death rates...Not surprisingly, there have been increasing indications of public discontent and voter dissatisfaction with the course of the reforms in the vast majority of countries.

The transition economies that boasted during the socialist era of total absence of poverty now openly acknowledged its existence, and showed concern over the new poor created by the transition. The countries of Eastern Europe of today are facing a three-fold challenge of: (i) stabilizing their economies, (ii) creating new institutions for functioning in the market-led economies, and (iii) thorough restructuring of their productive capacities to increase their efficiency in a competitive global market. In this process, the models of the West have been found to be deficient. That is why the International Commission on Peace and Food recommended that "rather than searching for a victor and the vanquished, the urgent need is to find a successor that combines and synthesises the enlightened values of both the systems". As a commercial, let me shed my modesty and recommend you to read my book titled *Poverty in Transition and Transition in Poverty* that analyzes the situation of social transformation in six countries of Eastern Europe. The case studies of these countries are quite revealing and they challenge the prevailing theories of poverty.

The same dilemma exists in the countries of the Third World to which India also belongs. Even when we tried to evolve a mixed economy, we have continually faltered on the social front. The recipe does not seem to have worked. World statistics suggest that the richest fifth of the world are appropriating 85 per cent of the global GNP, and the share of the poorest fifth is a meagre 1.4 per cent; the gap between the rich and the poor increased between 1960 and 1990 from 30:1 to 60:1 indicating unequal distribution of the dividends of economic and technological development. Such alarming disparity made people realize the shortcomings of the prevailing paradigm of development and express the need for a new prescription for the chronic ailment and a new blueprint for the world of the Third Millennium. This would require careful thinking, and a holistic approach in place of the clinical. To appreciate this better let us see what kind of social crisis we are currently facing. And I choose India to illustrate this point.

The India of 1947, when we became independent, was only 16 per cent literate. Regarding literacy as the key to development and a guarantee to modernization, we enthusiastically pursued the goal of universalization of education. But what happened? This year's budget proposes to launch a *"Sarva Shiksha Abhiyan"*—a movement to promote Education for All indicating that there continues to be deficit on this score. Over these years, we could only make 61 per cent of our people literate. This means that the number of illiterates today is as large as was the total population of India at the time of her independence; while in percentage terms we have made gains in literacy, in terms of actual numbers we still have an enormous size of illiterates—three times the size of Pakistan.

Despite the rising rate of literacy not only do we have a huge backlog of illiterates, we have also not been able to solve the problems of poverty and unemployment. The transformation that has taken place has changed the social profiles of the poor and the unemployed, adding the categories of educated poor and educated unemployed. The statistics are baffling. Worldwide, the size of the illiterates stands at 980 million, and that of the poor at 1.3 billion and constantly increasing. In India, the percentage of those below the poverty line is variously estimated between 15 and 39 per cent, whereas illiteracy percentage is around 39 per cent. Both these figures question the assumed causative relationship between education and poverty. This datum is a crude reminder that education alone is not able to solve the problems of poverty and unemployment. We must ask as to what effects does poverty have on education and what effects does education have on poverty. Elsewhere I have argued that we must identify various levels and forms of poverty and the various levels of educational attainment to relate the two. It is also to be remembered that while poverty is an attribute of the family—and not of an individual, or of a community or caste as a whole—education is a personal attribute. From this angle, the scheduled castes and scheduled tribes cannot be regarded as homogeneous population segments. Each caste and tribe is a socially differentiated structure in terms of these two attributes and therefore does not allow administration of a single prescription. The band-aid measures may look attractive but are hardly a substitute for careful medication or even a surgery. And we must speak this out, and substantiate through concrete research.

This is time now also to examine what the process of modernization has done to caste and ethnic groups. These groups are increasingly losing their core attributes of being endogamous groups and practitioners of hereditary occupation with growing phenomenon of intercaste (both intra- and inter-*varna*) marriages and heterogeneous occupational profiles of their members. At the same time, they are getting politicized thanks to the efforts of political parties. In the name of secularism, the political parties have encouraged these groups to assert their identities at the caste cluster level. Caste is thus dying in terms of its core attributes but is getting revived on a secular plank. We must acknowledge that the concern of sociologists and anthropologists in the investigation of caste has also contributed to this process. Remember the seminal essay of Professor Srinivas on the concept of dominant caste where he introduced the idea of "vote bank". This has become a part of political jargon. Few amongst us who questioned the assumptions of the dominant caste have regretfully been ignored. The election results exploding the myth of the vote bank notwithstanding, political analysts and social scientists find the category of caste convenient to their superficial explanation. We need good sociological studies of the election process to halt propagation of wrong perspectives and document the social transformation of caste. Both education and democracy—the two elements of the modernity syndrome—have contributed to the persistence of caste, and strangely enough in the name of secularism.

In a similar fashion, technological revolution, particularly communication revolution—yet another indicator of modernization—has been instrumental in fostering traditional and religious values. Consider the enormous impact of the TV serials—Mahabharata and Ramayana; these have carried the mythological messages to the Indians not only in India but also all over the world, thus binding them together in a cultural core; the migratory Indians regarded as modernists are returning to their traditional heritage via the medium of advanced technology. This phenomenon again has thrown the previous prescription that technology would replace tradition. Those who began writing the obituary of tradition are wonderstruck by its resilience.

Modern technology has not only brought the North to the countries of the South but also helped in registering the presence of the South in the countries of the North. It is this new phenomenon of international migration that has given rise to multiculturalism. The ancient civilization of India has always been pluricultural, but now with the migrants from the South the North is also becoming pluricultural and is getting alerted to this new social transformation. I have analyzed this emerging trend and have proposed the concept of *sandwich cultures* to investigate this phenomenon. I am glad that Professor Surendra Gupta of the Punjabi University, Patiala, has published already a full-length monograph on *Indians in Thailand* using my conceptual framework. Another scholar is using it in his investigation of the Trinidad society. This seems to me to be a very promising field of research.

In a speech like this, I can only be telegraphic in outlining an orientation. Let me hope that this seminar will deliberate upon some of the issues that I have raised and will suggest an agenda for research on social transformation. I must stress the need for well-planned empirical research on the processes of social transformation in India to give a solid base for planning and action. This would mean reviving our interest in the studies of the village and caste with a fresh perspective, and pushing the frontiers of our discipline to carry out researches on problems of poverty, unemployment, empowerment, and nation building in the context of multiculturalism.

The society expects from us sincere contributions of scientific nature. We must accept the challenge.

12

Sociology and the Future[*]

I thank you for the honour you have done me by asking me to deliver the valedictory address.

Usually such addresses are delivered by seniors in the profession, who use the opportunity to counsel the youngsters and wish them well. They have a whole past to draw upon, and are on the verge of leaving the stage. My position is peculiar; I am in the middle-range, a mixture of black and gray. And I do not intend to use this occasion to announce my retirement.

In the world of knowledge we make departures to arrive at newer crossroads; at times such destinations are preplanned and known, but at times they are quite serendipitous. We are also meeting here today to depart, hopefully not only in the physical sense. The tumultuous, brainstorming sessions of the past two days must have triggered new ideas and imaginations, and some of us might be returning with a fresh resolve to investigate newer research territories. My tributes to such resolves, and my best wishes for a period of hard and sustained work that will be needed to meet the challenges that you have picked up at this conference. We will all look forward to the new arrivals in sociological theory and research, that your departures will make possible.

---

* Valedictory address delivered at the All India Sociological Conference held in Surat in 1984, and published in the \i International Social Science Journal, \plain \f1 XXXVIII, No. 2, 1986, pp. 303-10.

I have deliberately used the language of mobility—departures and arrivals—to preface my address, in which I propose to dwell on tasks and challenges for sociology in the coming years, not only in India but in the region of Asia.

We are living in a mobile world, which is experiencing an unprecedented series of events: enormous population growth with the shortening of the doubling period; tremendous advances in science and technology, particularly in the field of communication, informatics, and in robotics; fast depletion of world resources, coupled with increasing demand for energy to meet the needs of newly industrializing countries in addition to those which are already industrialized; the evergrowing crisis of environmental pollution that may, at some stage, also engulf small and least developed countries when they join the industrial club; the threat of nuclear holocaust that presently governs the pattern of international relationships. Mass media are already terrorizing the world with their exhibition of "war games" and prefabrication of the scenario of "the day after" the N-bomb is released. We are told that 17th century was the century for mathematics, 18th saw the rise of physical sciences, 19th belonged to biological sciences, but the 20th century is a century of fear. The context of fear and uncertainty of the present and the coming century has brought social sciences to the fore. Perhaps this is what Comte meant when he proposed his hierarchy of sciences.

Intellectual climate the world over is obsessed with the future. There is disappointment with the past, and there is a fear of the future. Our todays are being guided by our tomorrows, and not by our yesterdays. Glorification of the past may be in conformity with our cultural instinct for ancestor worship; but we will train our coming generations only for obsolescence if we do not look ahead. In fact, the future is already with us; it is knocking at our doors. We are only realizing our incapability and helplessness to confront it. Do we adopt an attitude of resignation? Or do we stand up to take on the challenge?

When I say this, I speak in the spirit of self-searching and not with a view to criticize "others". I wish to emphasize the need for defining the role of social sciences in general, and of sociology in particular, in this newer context where global concerns and problems have become everyone's cup of tea.

There is, however, a need to dissect the global problems to see their regional and local manifestations. This is true both of the concerns of mankind, and concerns of the individual disciplines. What may appear frightening in global terms may be of peripheral concern to a small land-locked country, or to a remotely located village in a big country like India. Take for example, the question of environment. There is a basic difference in the environmental situation of our societies and that of the Western industrial societies. The developed societies are polluted societies; they are already suffering from suffocation caused by constant pollution of their environment. Our societies, still on the development path, have not reached the peak point of pollution; pollution, in our case, is still a peripheral problem, a problem of our metropolitan centres inhabited by a small percentage of our population. Viewed thus, for them—i.e., the Western societies—it is of immediate concern to solve the problem of pollution that affects almost all their population; for us, it is a warning for the future—if we continue industrializing we will suffer from fuel shortage on the one hand, and we will have polluted our environment, on the other. The Western societies, it seems, have reached a point of no return, and are perhaps not in a position to de-industrialize; they are, therefore, attempting such solutions as will not kill their factories and industries, and yet will not lead to further pollution. In case of the societies of the developing world, prescriptions are being offered for deschooling, for an extra-industrial path of development, for alternative strategies, for "appropriate" technologies. All this means that the list of priorities for research in our case has to be different; if we copy what is fashionable in the developed world we will be responding to their needs and not to our requirements.

The same is true of the global concerns in the social sciences as intellectual disciplines. The world profile of social sciences will list several achievements in the field of conceptualization, theory building, and methodology, and these would reflect largely the contributions of our Western peers who have been in the game for long. That is the reason that our colleagues in the West are engaged in the battle of paradigms, and in the pursuit of researches on topics that may not be regarded by us as of immediate relevance. But the Asian profile of sociology, as also of other social science disciplines, will not tally with this description. In Asia, we are still a much younger discipline, and we have still not been able to fully overcome the trauma of colonization which created a dependency syndrome. No doubt, we quite often hear the call for indigenization, but we have not gone beyond articulating our reactions against the intellectual kit that we have borrowed from the West. There is a manifestation of anger and ambivalence but there is little by way of concrete evidence of any replacement theories and methodology, if that is what indigenization really means. Of course, there is a certain revolution of relevance, a definite ascendancy of indigenous scholarship, more research being carried out by the so-called "insiders", and there is in evidence an opening of dialogue between producers and users of research. But even in case of these indicators, the picture varies from country to country; in comparison, India stands out as an example of a mature social science enterprise. Sociology in India has an Indian face and can take pride in having produced some sociologists of world renown.

The twin processes of decolonization and development have influenced the growth of sociology in India. In the initial phase, like other colonies, Indian society also provided a field laboratory for the outside scholarship. Studies of Indian society by outsiders began earlier than teaching of sociology and social anthropology in India. The second phase came when outsiders were joined by the insiders both in research and teaching, but the latter were still in minority. The third phase reversed the demographic composition: more insiders and less outsiders. With the advent of independence this pattern of insider-outsider interaction got drastically changed. During the colonial regime, there prevailed a *single-aperture model*: all external influences arrived via the flood-gate of the colonizer country; in the post-independent phase, the interaction began to be governed by a *multiple-aperture model*: influences flowed in from a wide variety of external settings.

Today we are no longer a recipient of ideas from a single source, namely the United Kingdom; scholarly transactions with other countries have increased with considerable reduction in such interchanges with the previous colonial master. In the process, some apertures did become bigger and an alert was sounded for a possible growth of academic colonialism, returning to a situation similar to the single-aperture model. That it did not happen, and that sociology in India has been able to withstand such an onslaught, is a point of enormous importance.

But let us not be complacent. We have a dual responsibility of protecting ourselves from the danger of recolonization of our minds on the one hand, and of chauvinistic insulation, on the other. It will be fatal to keep our doors closed. We should let outsiders also investigate our society and complement what we as insiders are able to achieve; similarly, we should also take on the "outsider" role and go out to study societies other than India, perhaps the societies of those outsiders who have frequented our terrain. This is the only way that we can deparochialize theory and contribute to the universality criterion of a science. The answer to parochial theories of the West is not production of yet another set of parochial theories of the Orient, but the fusion and sifting of the two through a process of deparochialization. Both the urge for a universal social science and the need to assist the development process, require free flow of communication across disciplines, to promote interdisciplinarity in our orientation. In the field of knowledge one does not engineer *coup d'état* to dethrone a discipline and take over the reins. What is "get-togethers" and not "takeovers". It is also in this sense in addition to other epistemological reasons, that the practitioners of sociology and social anthropology should not attempt to dig ditches to separate each other. That entire debate is futile and may be relegated to the realm of academic politics. Social sciences in the developing Third World have a long and arduous agenda; they can ill-afford the luxury of raising superficial issues related to disciplinary boundaries.

As I said in the beginning, the present intellectual mood is characterized by two concerns: our dissatisfaction with the past, and our concern for the future. It is this mood which is going to shape the sociology of the coming years. Let me briefly dwell upon this.

As we are coming nearer to the end of the present century, we are getting more and more concerned about inventorizing our achievements, on the one hand, and about the future shape of things, on the other. In the previous decades we were asked what we could do to assist the development process, and we responded to the call by beginning to reorientate our studies towards social and cultural change; as our economist friends participated directly in the planning process at the macro level, we turned our eyes towards the micro settings—the village communities—and studied their social structures as well as the impact on them of the forces of directed cultural change and of the winds of modernization. For posterity we have succeeded in preserving the descriptions of those communities that will no longer be the same. As development proceeded, we began discovering many unanticipated consequences. For most of these consequences economists and technocrats put the blame on the "tradition", and culture was declared as the key culprit.

To fight back, we defended the cultures and declared planners to be guilty of wrong prescriptions, and held administrators responsible for mismanagement. This is intellectual wrestling and mud smearing. The answer to this impasse is not a matter of two words. It invites our attention to a thorough re-examination of the entire exercise, and careful planning of development effort in the future.

Let us acknowledge that development is a continuing concern of the contemporary world. That is why the United Nations launched its Third Development Decade in January 1981 despite the frustration caused by the fact that "the goals and objectives of the International Development Strategy for the Second Development Decade remain largely unfulfilled" and that the world economy experienced a series of negative trends. The call for the establishment of a New International Economic Order made fervently during the last decade has again been reaffirmed. The world community is firmly resolved to do whatever it can, to better the lot of more than 850 million people in the countries of the Third World who are living at the margin of existence. Development has a meaning only when this happens. It is a war against want, and like any war, it requires a strategy that works.

The grim recognition of the failure of the original paradigm of development, that laid emphasis on economic growth, has led the intellectual community to a post-mortem of the experiment and to the formulation of alternatives. From a single approach we are moving towards a multitude of approaches; from unilinearity implied in the earlier paradigm there is a growing acceptance of multilinearity in development; from sectoral emphases there is a departure towards strategies for integrated development. It is in this process that old concerns are now seen in new light. To be sure, there were poor in the 1950s and 1960s, and there were also vast masses living in rural areas during that period, and there were programmes of rural development and of removal of poverty. But one notices the return of the very same concerns in the late 1970s and 1980s. Consider how often we now recite the words "poverty" and "rural development". It is a testimony to the failure of development that economic growth has not been painless, that it has further crippled the poor and has inflicted injuries on the rural populations. We are led to believe that local and national development cannot be assured by a single replicative global paradigm, that global development is dependent on local and national development, that an overemphasis on homogenization is an enemy of development, and that forces of endogenous development need to be fostered rather than mutilated.

Rethinking on development has not been confined to the developing world, however. Even the treatment of the West as "reference group" has been questioned, not only by the scholars of the Third World but also internally by critics from the developed world itself. One of the authors, for example, has pointed out that in the richest countries of the world, which represent only 10 per cent of the world population, there is "98 per cent of the world's psycho-pharmacological consumption, 86 per cent of impotency and frigidity, 86 per cent of telephone calls, 80 per cent of suicides, 78 per cent of television consumption, 74 per cent of heart attacks" and so on. These are the countries which are characterized by endogenous development using the industrial paradigm, and also emphasizing the man-centred concept of development.

When one listens today to the slogan for endogenous development, he cannot help but feel cautious about its implications. One may as well ask whether it is the same old recipe under a new label. In order to make these concepts of "endogenous development" and "keeping the man in the centre" relevant and useful as elements of the new strategy there is a need to invest in them a new and different meaning. As Johan Galtung and his co-authors have pointed out there are three fallacies of a man-centred concept of development, namely, anthropocentrism, Eurocentrism, and psychological reductionism. The authors quite rightly say that a "new concept of man-centred development requires a new relationship between man and nature, one that is less exploitative and domineering". Further, the "ideal man-centred development is one that provides room for individual emancipation but gives priority to group solidarity and collective decision-making". It is also important to realize that Eurocentrism led us to believe that the theories emanating from the West are "universal"; that they are not is proven by the experience of the developing countries.

The experience of the last 20 years has made us a bit sober; we feel less definite about the future than before. We have come to realize that mere money and machines are not enough for a society to develop, and that variety and diversity have their own virtues. Already there are scholars who are busy developing blueprints for alternative strategies to attain the developmental goal. Governments are engaged in experimenting with new ideas for local-level planning and people's involvement. In India, one can come across several examples of such an effort; to quote a few: escalated irrigation programme, guaranteed employment approach, food for work programme, Antyodaya (or redemption of the very last), milk scheme or Operation Flood, and the special small farmer development scheme. One can recount similar efforts in other countries of the region. It is schemes such as these, rather than grandiose theories, that are bringing development nearer to the people.

Efforts are also afoot at the global level to develop designs for alternative restructuring of the international system of relationships. The famous Brandt report published under the title "North-South: A Programme for Survival" is a good example of an exercise that has stirred people's minds. Professor Rajni Kothari has written *Footsteps into the Future*. Dr. Leontif has discussed the *Future of the World Economy*. Lestar Brown of the Worldwatch Institute has invited our attention to the need for *Building a Sustainable Society* by reciting the famous French riddle of the 29th day. Earlier, the world has been told of the *Limits to Growth* by the Club of Rome, and was advised by Schumacher that *Small is Beautiful*.

We have begun the Third Development Decade with the rediscovery of issues. As one of the World Bank studies states: "It is now considered that maximization of GNP per capita is too narrow an aim and that other aims related of poverty reduction need to be considered as well: improving income distribution, increasing employment, fulfilling basic needs". The study says that the recent heightened concern with eradication of poverty is not likely....to be just another fad. On the contrary, in the long run it is the narrow preoccupation of the late 1950s and 1960s with growth in average per capita income that....may turn out to be the passing fashion".

It seems clear that the answer to our present crisis does not lie in the replacement of the old paradigm by another single recipe. Each nation and society has to work out its own strategy of development that would answer its needs and be appropriate in its context. There is also need to discard measuring development by a single yardstick of dollar value and to employ instead the concept of "purchasing power parities". It is in many ways misleading to say that 12 Indian rupees, for example, are roughly one US dollar. By such reduction we only succeed in placing ourselves in perpetual poverty compared to an external referent. Some calculations based on the concept of purchasing power parity suggest that India's per capita income is close to US $450 rather than $140 as conventionally measured.

Rethinking development is essentially an exercise in thinking for the future. There is concern to ensure that we are not caught unawares and ushered into a future that we do not want. It is a call for the preparation for the future.

An agenda for future depends upon our power of prediction. It is paradoxical that with the growth of knowledge this power has weakened and not strengthened. To give one example: with all the advances in science and technology, and with the available tools to handle enormous empirical data, we were unable to predict the shortage of oil that virtually crippled the world for a while and forced scientists and technologists to discover alternative sources of renewable energy. Shortage of oil was not a mere geological question; it became an element in international politics and resulted in the secular assertion of Islamic power. The magnet of petrodollar introduced a remarkably different phenomenon of international migration which made it possible for many villagers from Asia to jump from bullock cart to a jumbo jet, and return home after a couple of years with money and modern material culture to begin a new style of life. The tourist industry in Asia has been affected by the Sheikh tourists from the Middle East. It is they, and not the Indo-Pak travellers who have promoted Indian restaurants throughout the region—a phenomenon which is only 5-6 years old.

In relatively "no-change", or "slow-change" societies, the future was more or less predictable. Socialization in them was only a matter of transmitting tradition from older generation to the younger. But in the climate of change we have become less certain about the future, and this has posed a serious challenge to the processes of socialization. It is a strain on our imagination to perceive the future, which will be the result of a combination of a wide variety of factors—both internal and external—at a given social system.

In the literature on future, two trends are easily discernible. There are those who despair with the past and the present and prescribe a new blueprint for the future which would require a revolutionary effort. Then there are those who extrapolate the emerging trends and indicate shocking proportions of the problem by the year 2000 or any other future referral point.

The first set of scholars, the utopia builders, show us an optimistic garden path; the second set of scholars provide us with the warning signals. Then there is yet another group of scholars who are mesmerized by the rapid advances made in technology and who have assumed the role of persuasive salesmen for its adoption and promotion of efforts to further its cause. Computers have already become a commodity for personal domestic use. As if Apple Computers was not small enough, we will soon be provided with "peanuts". Knowledge contained in an encyclopaedia will be made available on a micro chip, smaller than the size of the back of our palm; such strides will replace the staircase theory of evolution, not by the "escalator" principle, but by the new concept of "leap-frogging". They are convinced that there is no going back, nor is there any other path possible.

A whole series of new assumptions are at work: inevitability of technological growth; dawn of an information society which will make it possible to establish dialogues between machines, and leave man with more time for leisure; there is even going to be "artificial intelligence". But such scenarios are global at best; such things may be happening somewhere in the world and therefore it may represent a newer stage of development in the world civilization. However, there is not going to be a single future for all the societies of the world. We have to think of future as a plural; of several futures. The amount of energy that will be needed for the entire world to have a technological and information society, such as Japan, or USA, is simply not available nor could it possibly be generated; that is why people are talking about a low-energy society in a high energy world.

In thinking about the future, not in the style of a utopian who prescribes a complete overhaul, we will, in my view, have to identify three different elements of the situation. One, those aspects which will continue to persist, but which may increase or decrease in quantitative terms; two, those that are inevitable; and three, the unanticipated arrivals, be they disasters, revolutionary upheavals, or unintended consequences of many of our efforts. Each society will have a different structure of its future comprising these elements. It is our ability to foresee this structure that will determine our capabilities to cope with it.

I submit that there is no single orientation to the future. We still have people who think of a strategy for future essentially in terms of improvement from the present in order to "look alike" the "present", or even the "past" of some other successful societies. There are also those who would like to see their society different from others, and therefore, would like to return to the corridors of their cultural past to reintroduce forgotten values, revive religious beliefs, and establish a distinctive cultural identity through closure of apertures and installation of insulators. There are those who perceive what is going on, and on the basis of their assessment of prevalent trends suggest either a clinical approach to treat the disease or prescribe a prophylactic treatment to forestall a pathological encounter. There are those who accept the current trends as inevitable and irreversible and commend the need to retrain ourselves to meet the future needs. And of course, there are those who would like to take on the role of a modern "Manu" and prepare new "Smritis".

In many ways the question of "values" assumes special significance in an intellectual exercise on the future, because socialization for future requires some indoctrination and some skill formation. It seems hard to arrive at a consensus on a desirable future. It is quite possible that the features that appear shocking and demeaning to some may incite quite a different reaction among others. Even if there were a consensus on a desirable future and people succeed in fashioning such a future, it remains open to criticism by the coming generations for whom we will be building it. Our right choices may be regarded as wrong by them; they will have the benefit of hind sight to unravel our mistakes, as we are doing now vis-à-vis our predecessors.

It is in this context that I wish to raise questions regarding the teaching of sociology. Within academia people have begun raising issues related to education and future. The relationship between the two is variously described: education in future, contribution of education to future, preparation of the students for future, redesigning of educational apparatus to meet the demands of the future, and so on. The discussions have focussed both on defining education and its role, and profiling of the future.

At first glance, it may sound strange to raise a question of this nature because education implies preparation for future. The present-day school-going population is tomorrow's labour force. And it is the role of the school to prepare them for their future entry into the economy and polity in their roles. But this is no longer the case. With rapid changes taking place, the strategy of preparing students for a known future is not going to work anymore. Our specializations create in us "trained incapacities". And newer forms of incompetencies are being created.

We no longer talk of literacy alone. Education means both literacy and numeracy; some have added to it ecology, i.e., knowledge about the environment. With the invasion of computer culture, yet another qualification of computeracy has been added. One has to be a literate, numerate, ecolate, and a computerate to face the future generation of students who will have a better numerical sense, a well-trained algebraic faculty, and a facility to communicate with the electronic mill, that is, the computer. What we were taught as statistics in our M.A. is now learnt by a young child at school. We are reaching a stage in our education system where age and seniority may not remain the indices of knowledge superiority. Even schools, in many societies no longer are in a position to monopolize all learning. The phenomenon of "school compatibles" needs to be reckoned with. In many countries in Asia, children are acquiring their computer competence in toy shops; peers are turning out to be better teachers than the seniors. Thus, there are functional equivalents of school, and there are surrogate teachers.

One task of the education system is to notice this trend and develop a tradition of continuous updating of the curricula. The second task is to foresee the kinds of jobs that will be available to the students when they leave the portals of an academic institution. With the "idiot" of the computer coming handy, the task of "memorizing" can be easily assigned to it and the student can be trained more to think, to question, to experiment. He should be prepared to adapt himself to changing situations, and his skills should be such that can be used for a wide variety of challenges in the job market. He will need to be a generalist of a different calibre. Through various short-term training programmes for specific skills we have to build-up capabilities to handle long-term uncertainties. The third task is to anticipate the future student clientele and bring about transformation in the social structure and knowledge structure of the school. For one thing, despite the growth of school compatibles, the school is almost certainly not going to disappear. It will have more students, and it will be called upon to train them in a wide variety of skills. It is for us sociologists to realize the challenge that is inherent in these foreseeable changes. Not to talk of exercises in sociology of sociology, we have, particularly in India, not made much progress even in the sociology of school, or sociology of education. And it is time that we consider this matter seriously.

We face a future with a loss of our predictability in the wake of increasing complexities. We are experiencing an intense urge to fashion our future rather than to arrive at an unknown destination; we do not want to pursue the "look-alike" model to become a xerox copy of some other culture, and yet we cannot ignore the continuous onslaught of technology from which there is no going back. How do we reconcile our urge for cultural identity, with our concern for development, and our desire not to deny the fruits of science and technology which are part of a universal human "heritage"?

I am not one of those who subscribe to the view that our future can be built on the ashes of the present. I believe our future will be a consequence of what we do now. While thinking about fashioning a desirable future, I would like to ask the following questions:

1. Will the future generation accept our definition of the "desirable" society?
2. Should we try to build unshakable edifices of the future society or should we leave sufficient scope for the coming generations to reject what they might describe as our follies, and to renovate and reconstruct the society according to their own needs and values?
3. Should we treat our present as an inheritance from our ancestors, or as something that we have borrowed from our yet-to-be-born great grandchildren?

These are not easy questions to answer and I leave them with you to ponder.

13

Indian Sociology: From Where to Where

Footnotes to the History of the Discipline*

A golden jubilee is an occasion for celebration. It is also perhaps an occasion for reflection on the journey covered so far, and for developing a new road map for further excursions. I recall a similar ceremony held in 1969 when the department of sociology at the Bombay University completed its fiftieth year of existence. That occasion was celebrated in the form of a national seminar on the general theme of "Modernization"—the "in-thing" at that time in Indian sociology. Two stalwarts of modern sociology from Columbia University—Professor Robert K. Merton and Professor Paul F. Lazarsfeld, incidentally my teachers—came as special invitees to the seminar.

In a special lecture, Professor Merton dwelt on the phenomenon of "insiders and outsiders" as a problem in the

* The Indian Sociological Society, celebrating its Golden Jubilee at the XXVII All India Sociological Conference, held at the Guru Nanak Dev University, Amritsar, organized a special session on *The State of the Profession: Indian Sociology—Yesterday, Today, and Tomorrow*. Dr U.B. Bhoite chaired the session. Other speakers were Bula Bhadra, Karuna Chanana, and N. Jayaram. Since the organizers provided no guidelines, each speaker chose to speak on the area of her/his interest. Since I was called upon to initiate the discussion, I used the opportunity to develop a framework for exploring such a vast territory. Quite understandably, other speakers stuck to their prepared texts, and did not build upon my statement. Given here is the elaborated version of my initiatory remarks at the symposium.

area of sociology of knowledge. By choosing to elaborate on the twin concepts, which he had briefly developed as part of his theory of reference groups, he imaginatively focussed on a crucial problem in social science research of that time. In the United States, some black intellectuals were putting forward "most clearly and emphatically" the doctrine that "as a matter of social epistemology, *only* black historians can truly understand black history, *only* black ethnologists can understand black culture, *only* black sociologists can understand the social life of blacks and so on". Referring to the *de facto* "insiderism", Merton acknowledged: "It has simply taken the form of patterned expectations about the appropriate selection of specialties and of problems for investigation. The handful of Negro sociologists were in large part expected, as a result of social selection and self-selection, to study problems of Negro life and relations between the races just as the handful of women sociologists were expected to study the problems of women, principally as these related to marriage and the family" (1972:13). Aware of the Indian criticism of outsider research, and putting himself in the status of an "outsider" in the company of Indian sociologists, Merton said in the 1971 version of his paper (A.R. Desai, ed., 1971:456): "the social scientists of India...have long suffered the slings and arrows of outrageously unprepared and altogether exogenous social scientists engaging in swift, superficial inquiries into matters Indian". Just as he was examining the claim of the black sociologists, Merton obliquely invited Indian sociologists to rethink the question regarding the role of outsiders in understanding Indian society.

The debate about the definition of Indian sociology began in the 1950s when the discipline gained recognition in the academia, and its professionalization began. The holding of the All India Sociological Conference was the first indicator of sociology's independent existence. And, the debate was initiated by the presidential address delivered to the conference by Professor D.P. Mukerji at the First All India Sociological Conference, held in Dehradun in 1955. Mukerji's address emphasized the need for the study of tradition. He attributed the failure of social sciences to contribute to India's development "chiefly on account of their ignorance of and un-rootedness in India's social reality" (Mukerji, 1958: 234). His argument was that "greater ease of insight and understanding" can be "secured by the sociologist when he is saturated in his own traditions" (Ibid.: 232). Although Mukerji took care to qualify his statement by saying that he was not suggesting to bar "foreign scholars out of Indian problems", both Indian followers of Mukerji and his foreign critics interpreted him as an advocate of "insiderism". Some of his students took the call seriously and over-reacted by pleading a case for Indian sociology more or less divorced from its Western counterpart. Quite the opposite view was held by others, particularly those who had training in anthropology. For example, M.N. Srinivas believed that the insider is so "fundamentally and even hopelessly enslaved in one's society that detachment is well-nigh impossible. Such detachment is necessary if one wants to present an account of one's society which is intelligible to others... In fact, I would go so far as to maintain that the study of an alien society is a prerequisite to understanding one's own" (Srinivas, 1955:4). The two arguments in a way represented the distinction between the perspectives of sociology and anthropology—that sociology is the study of one's own society and anthropology of "other cultures".[1]

When Merton came to greet and bless his Indian counterparts in 1969, Indian sociology was still struggling to establish its separate identity, although it had completed its first fifty years. The debate on the distinction between sociology and social anthropology was rife in India, and the subject had just entered into a reactive phase against Western social science. The profession was coping with an identity crisis. Merton's seminal paper provided a meaningful frame of reference, and took the debate from the platform of academic politics to the arena of sociology of knowledge. However, those who wrote on the growth of the discipline in this country did not follow that lead, albeit his concepts of "outsiders" and "insiders" gained some currency in Indian writing.

Now, in the year 2001, we celebrate the fiftieth year of our association—the Indian Sociological Society. The theme chosen for this symposium has a time orientation—past, present and the future. It would have been ideal to have on this panel sociologists representing different age groups—those who have retired, to reflect on their times; those who are in the middle reaches or on the verge of retirement, to provide a bridge between the past and the future; and the new initiates who are readying themselves to take over. But such is not the composition of this panel. All the four speakers invited to this symposium are currently active. Although in terms of employment I have joined the ranks of the retired, I would like to place myself in the category of the "present continuous".

I am not sure where the "yesterday" ended, and from where we began our "today". Just as we are not sure of the beginning of our today, we are also left guessing about its becoming a yesterday when the "tomorrow" will turn into a "today". These are arbitrary boundaries.

Writers of the history of Indian sociology have used different schemes to classify the various periods.

L.P. Vidyarthi (1966), for example, talks of a "Formulatory Period" from 1774 through 1919; "Constructive Period" from 1920 through 1949; and "Analytical Period" from 1950 onwards.

In a study for UNESCO prepared by D.N. Dhanagare (1984)[2], the various phases of the development of Indian sociology are recounted thus: the colonial heritage, indigenous social thought and renaissance, institutionalization: pre-1950 phase, expansion of teaching and research; post-1950 period. In the last phase, Dhanagare has devoted a separate section on research trends between the years 1950-1979.

In a 1979 publication, titled *Sociology of Indian Sociology*, Ramkrishna Mukherjee identified growth points in terms of its practitioners whom he classified as pioneers, modernizers, insiders, and pace makers and non-conformists. He has made critical assessment of the contributions made by scholars belonging to these categories, and identifying the "insiders" emerging in the late sixties and seventies as those who were the product of the system rather than entrants from other disciplines.

Perhaps, the formulatory and constructive periods of Vidyarthi, or the period before 1950 in Dhanagare's periodization that included the colonial heritage, indigenous thought, and initial steps to introduce the discipline, or the period when Mukherjee's pioneers and modernizers occupied the centre stage, can be called our "yesterday". With few exceptions, all the stalwarts of that period are unfortunately gone. Ramkrishna Mukherjee's list of pioneers included A.K. Coomarswamy, B.N. Seal, B.K. Sarkar, G.S. Ghurye, D.P. Mukerji, Radhakamal Mukerjee, S.V. Ketkar, B.N. Dutt, and K.P. Chattopadhyay; among modernizers mention is specifically made of M.N. Srinivas, S.C. Dube, R.N. Saksena, D.N. Majumdar, I.P. Desai, K.M. Kapadia and their contemporaries. Mukherjee has called them "modernizers" in the sense that the "majority of sociologists who appeared in society at this time shared the ideology of the policy makers and the corresponding practice of the policy promoters" (1979:47). These scholars followed a pragmatic approach and focussed on empirical research. From studies of the social structures of the local communities they moved towards the changing scene.[3] Srinivas' concepts *of sanskritization* and *Westernization* were widely used, discussed, and debated.[4]

From this, I would take the clue and propose that the post-Srinivas and post-Dube period—represented by the people of my generation that has crossed (or is crossing) the line of 60—marks the beginning of Indian sociology's "today". In terms of Ramkrishna Mukherjee's classification, we may fall into the category of "insiders", though I would hesitate to accept that label.

The time when people of my generation entered the profession, an insider culture began to develop in Indian sociology with self-employed gatekeepers restricting the entry to those who had formal degrees in the discipline. Questions were raised even about the eligibility of persons like S.C. Dube (who had B.A. Honours in political science and a Ph.D. in social anthropology[5]), R.N. Saksena and Brij Raj Chauhan (sociology graduates from the Lucknow University having their M.A. degrees in economics). Trained in social anthropology, people like us had the status of the marginalized. Physical anthropologists, and even those calling themselves general anthropologists regarded us as "deserters" and the fellow sociologists treated us as "intruders".

Some others having formal training in sociology also felt like "outsiders" because of the treatment meted out to them. For example, Dhanagare and Oommen, who were sociology graduates from Nagpur and Pune respectively, chose to describe themselves as outsiders albeit for different reasons. Dhanagare called himself an "outsider within" (Dhanagare, 1993:13). "Not being a product", he says, "of either the Lucknow School, the Bombay School, or the Delhi School, which were the leading centres of training in sociology in the late 1950s when I studied...Subsequently...I got the opportunity to study at the University of Sussex and completed a work which belongs in the gray area between comparative sociology and social history" (Ibid.). Dhanagare, however, asserts that "professionally I always identified myself with the community of sociologists though with a self-imposed marginal status...To that extent, my status as an 'outsider within' in Indian sociology offered me some latent advantage whereby I could detach and distance myself from the mainstream of the sociology profession without being totally alienated from it the same time" (Ibid.). In his article on "Insiders and Outsiders: Primordial Collectivism and Cultural Pluralism in Nation Building"[6] Oommen alleges that he has been treated as an "outsider" by the "mainstream social science" that is dominated, according to him, by the Hindus and Hindiwallas. He feels jubilant while asserting that despite such resistance he has reached the core of Indian sociology. It is interesting to note that Dhanagare started his career as a civil servant in Maharashtra and later entered the profession with his appointment at the Institute of Social Sciences, Agra University. Similarly, Oommen had to leave Jaipur to gain an entry as sociology teacher at the Delhi School of Social Work and not at the Delhi School of Economics, which had set up a department of sociology under the chairmanship of Professor Srinivas.[7] And Professor Srinivas who was regarded as a social anthropologist, with his Oxford degree and international recognition, had very little to do with the department of anthropology of Delhi University. He recruited social anthropologist, Andre Beteille—with a degree from Calcutta University—to teach sociology in his own department. By any standard, all these scholars are very much "insiders" to the profession. Even the self-proclaimed outsiders—Oommen and Dhanagare—have been elected to the high office of the President of the Indian Sociological Society. Oommen also became the President of the International Sociological Association.

Srinivas and Dube represent that class of social anthropologists who did not make any distinction between sociology and social anthropology. In fact, they worked for their close collaboration. There were other social anthropologists who clamoured for an independent status. In sociology also, there were many who resented entry of social anthropologists. Interestingly, the scholars who belonged to the so-called "Lucknow School" exhibited this ambivalence because that university had well-established departments of both the disciplines. It is of historical interest to note that Dube succeeded in creating a joint department of sociology and anthropology at the University of Sagar in the 1960s. But after his departure from Sagar, internal politics led to the bifurcation of the disciplines into two separate departments—both headed by his own students. What is more distressing is the fact that the Sagar department of anthropology today does not have any permanent teacher in social anthropology! As against this, at the University of Rajasthan, a professorship in anthropology was created in the 1980s where I was invited to deliver the inaugural lecture pending the appointment to the chair.

The insider-outsider duality in the profession has influenced the growth of the discipline. As we look back we may say that such debates have lost relevance today. But it is instructive to note that the outsider status had four distinct connotations: (i) those not having formal degrees in the discipline of sociology and entering as pioneers, (ii) those having degrees in social anthropology (T.N. Madan, Andre Beteille, Yogesh Atal) but open to the exposure to sociology, (iii) those not belonging to the established schools of sociology and thus facing difficulties in gaining entry into the profession, and (iv) those non-conformists—kept away from the so-called "mainstream sociology" (followers of the Marxist approach or those belonging to the non-Hindu, non-Hindi group of sociologists). A mention should also be made of yet another category of outsiders, namely the expatriate researchers working on India. It is interactions with them that sharpened the debate on the definition of "Indian sociology". Apart from several national seminars, that debate was carried on in the pages of the *Contributions to Indian Sociology*. That debate was both about the content and orientation of the discipline and about its practitioners. The *Contributions* was started by Louis Dumont and David Pocock, and later handed over to T.N. Madan who recently took retirement. As the name of the journal suggests, *Contributions* was, and is, primarily an outlet for publishing contributions of foreign (outsider) sociologists and anthropologists to Indian sociology. This is not to suggest that the journal did not publish any Indian contributions; the point is that it is not representative of contributions made by Indians to Indian sociology. A better source for the latter is the *Sociological Bulletin* and *Eastern Anthropologist.* There is no place here to go into detail, but clearly these distinctions are a part of the academic politics within the discipline. Sociology as it stands today has been enriched by the contributions of all such outsiders who are now treated as insiders.

Professionalization of the discipline began with the establishment of the Indian Sociological Society by those belonging to the Bombay School. The Society had a journal but did not succeed much in organizing conferences. Parallel to this, those belonging to the Lucknow School took the initiative to organize All India Sociological Conferences that were attended by people from all over India, including those who were members of the Indian Sociological Society (ISS). Six such conferences were held in which the sessions were divided into sociology, social anthropology, social psychology, and statistics and research methodology. Those conferences can easily be called social science conferences with participation of sociologists, anthropologists, psychologists and statisticians. Later, the two initiatives were merged and the conferences held prior to the merger were counted as conferences of the ISS.

We have certainly come a long way. The Indian Council of Social Science Research (ICSSR) published in the 1970s the first set of three volumes surveying the research done on different aspects of sociology and social anthropology in India—an endeavour with which I was personally associated in my capacity as Director of Sociology at the ICSSR in those days. ICSSR also launched a Journal of Research Abstracts and Reviews around that time, with T.N. Madan as its editor. There have been updates of the surveys of research that tell of the journey so far covered by Indian sociology. A bibliographic index of articles and book reviews published in the *Sociological Bulletin* provides yet another source[8] to document the history of development of sociology in this country. It can be used to identify trends and shifts in emphasis, as well as arrival of new themes and specialties in the profession. Apart from this, that publication of the ISS can also be used to detect the elements of professional politics—to verify the charge of marginalization by the so-called "mainstream" sociology. It is interesting to note that while Oommen complains of an "outsider treatment" by the mainstream, he figures as one of the oft published authors of the bulletin. The outgoing President of the Indian Sociological Society—B.S. Baviskar—described that index as a "Who's Who of Indian Sociology". While this is true in the sense that practically all those who matter in the profession find a mention, but not so in terms of frequency. Amongst the least published authors would figure the names of giants like S.C. Dube. Very few of his books have been reviewed in the *Sociological Bulletin*. When I looked at the entries against my name, I was not surprised to find that only one of my books out of several that I authored or edited has been reviewed, and two of my articles and two reviews done by me have been published; in my long career until 1999 I have refereed only one article. From this angle, one can easily find the core group that monopolized the *Sociological Bulletin* and the ISS notwithstanding some exceptions. It was perhaps the growing resentment against such a monopoly that the recent elections to the society snatched away all key positions from Delhi. As we look back on our yesterday and the continuing today perhaps this aspect of Indian sociology needs to be studied sociologically. Ramkrishna Mukherjee's book makes an impressive start in this direction, as the title of the book suggests—*Sociology of Indian Sociology*. But there is much that remains to be done.

Available histories of the discipline have focussed more on how sociology arrived on the Indian scene and what problems it encountered in gaining recognition within the academe. But there is a need to focus on how the discipline, in its next phase of consolidation and independent identity became insulated, and how various departments became endogamous by valuing ascribed status of "department product" and virtually closing the doors for those "born elsewhere". The consequences of such "insiderism" need to be investigated. Such insiderism was confined not only to recruitments but also to exclusion of outside contributions. There is not only a tendency to quote the foreigners, but to deliberately ignore the works of Indian peers, and particularly the juniors especially when they are not the "insiders".

In the last two-three decades, new frontiers have opened in the discipline with the marriages between, for example, economics and sociology, political science and sociology, and history and sociology. These have brought in interdisciplinary perspective and helped develop specialisms in economic sociology, political sociology, and historical sociology. Opening of these new frontiers have broken some insulations and created fresh apertures to bring fresh light and refreshing ideas from the outside. Similarly, the emerging focus on movements, on gender issues, and on environmental concerns has necessitated an interdisciplinary, even transdisciplinary perspective. Our assessment of Indian sociology of today ought to reflect on them.

While contemplating on the footsteps into the future, it is necessary not only to highlight the achievements of the past, or glorify the works of our ancestors, but also to go beyond. To quote Alfred North Whitehead: "A science which hesitates to forget its founders is lost". We should heed the call of Robert Merton to distinguish between history and "systematics of theory". We need such exercises that "would take up such matters as the complex filiation of sociological ideas, the ways in which they developed, the connections of theory with the changing social origins and subsequent social statuses of its exponents, the interaction of theory with the changing social organization of sociology, the diffusion of theory from centres of sociological thought and its modification in the course of diffusion, and the ways in which it was influenced by changes in the environing culture and social structure. The distinction put into practice would, in short, make for a sociological history of sociological theory" (Merton, 1967:2). I feel time has come when we should attempt synthesis of available findings from a myriad field studies of microcosms, and assess Indian contribution to sociological theory and to research methodology. Indian sociologists have contributed to the conceptual kit, have offered refinements to the theories—for example, reference group theory through work on the processes of modernization and sanskritization, and on dominant caste; on nation building; migration; multiculturalism; insider-outsider duality. All these need to be culled out from various monographs and papers and properly synthesized.

At the same time, our preparation for the tomorrow should include fresh prioritization of our research agenda. The stocktaking exercises give us enough clues of the research gaps that exist in terms of themes not properly covered or regions of the country not investigated. Even the areas or groups that were studied earlier require a revisit to see the changes that have taken place in their social structures and cultures. New methodologies, and techniques supported by the "machine culture" can yield fresh data and enable us to attempt sophisticated analyses. Issues related to environment, social development, migration, multiculturalism, ageing, impact of information technology, and research of crisis situations such as earthquakes are the areas that await good sociological studies.

I strongly feel that our tomorrows should shape our todays. We may build on our yesterdays, but should also make a solid foundation for our tomorrows. The yesterdays can make us complacent, but the future throws up the challenge. It is less important to talk about the point of our departure in the past, we must think of our next destination. Not where did we come from, but where do we go from here.

Notes

1. In my other essays in this volume I have dwelt at length on this issue.
2. *Sociology and Social Anthropology in Asia and the Pacific* (edited by Yogesh Atal), Wiley Eastern, New Delhi and UNESCO, Paris, 1984.
3. Mukherjee cites the title of S.C. Dube's second book on rural India, *India's Changing Villages,* as an apt description of the changing focus. See p.52.
4. There is a recent trend to include some others as pioneers. For example, Bela Dutt (1972: Chapter 111) Gupta attempts to install Rammohan Roy, Akshay Kumar Dutta, Pandit Ishwar Chandra Vidyasagar, Pyari Chand Mitra, Kaliprasanna Sinha, Bhudev Mukherjee all from Bengal, and Vishnu Bhikaji Gokhale of Maharashtra in the list of founding fathers. The striking example, however, is the mention of a freedom fighter Shyamji Krishna Verma about whom B.K. Nagla says that he met Auguste Comte in Europe; the fact of the matter is that Comte died in the year 1857 when Verma was born ! (See NCERT book on *Introducing Sociology,* 2002, page 3). All such attempts are "adumbrationist" to use Merton's coinage.
5. I recall when I proposed his name for an examinership in social anthropology in the Panjab University, the then Head of the department questioned his credentials! I had to tell him that if Dube was not competent to be an examiner in anthropology, I should be disqualified to teach the subject.
6. See Yogesh Atal (ed.), *Understanding Indian Society,* Har-Anand Publications, New Delhi, 1992, Chapter 20.

7. Incidentally, the same year (1961) I was also appointed Assistant Professor of Sociology at the Agra University, thus moving from anthropology to sociology. The same Selection Committee chose me and Dhanagare.
8. 50 Years of *Sociological Bulletin* (Journal of the Indian Sociological Society) 1952-2001. Index compiled by Krishnan Namboodiri, Indian Sociological Society, New Delhi, 2001.

References

Atal, Yogesh, 1976, *Social Sciences: The Indian Scene,* Abhinav Publications, New Delhi.

Atal, Yogesh (ed.), 1984, *Sociology and Social Anthropology in Asia and the Pacific* (ed. Yogesh Atal), Wiley Eastern, New Delhi and UNESCO, Paris.

Atal, Yogesh (ed.), 1992, *Understanding Indian Society,* Har-Anand Publications, New Delhi.

Dhanagare, D.N., 1993, *Themes ad Perspectives in Indian Sociology,* Rawat Publications, Jaipur.

Gupta, Bela Dutt, 1972, *Sociology in India,* Centre for Sociological Research, Calcutta.

Mukerji, D.P., 1958, *Diversities: Essays in Economics, Sociology and Other Social Problems,* People's Publishing House, New Delhi.

Mukherjee, Ramkrishna, 1979, *Sociology of Indian Sociology,* Allied Publishers, New Delhi.

Nayar, P.K.B. (ed.), 1982, *Sociology in India,* B.R. Publishing Corporation, Delhi.

Vidyarthi, L.P., 1966, "Anthropological Researches in India: Some Preliminary Observations", *Journal of Social Research,* Vol.IX, No. 1, March.

Index